SOUTH CAROLINA RULES OF EVIDENCE 2021

Complete Rules in Effect as of January 1, 2021

Convenient Briefcase Edition Perfect for the Courtroom or Office. Complete Rules in Effect as of January 1, 2021.

ISBN: 9798591919870

Peter Edwards, Esq.
South Carolina Legal Publishing, LLC

Table of Contents

Article I. General Provisions 5
- RULE 101. SCOPE 5
- RULE 102. PURPOSE AND CONSTRUCTION 5
- RULE 103. RULINGS ON EVIDENCE 6
- RULE 104. PRELIMINARY QUESTIONS 8
- RULE 105. LIMITED ADMISSIBILITY 10
- RULE 106. REMAINDER OF OR RELATED WRITINGS OR STATEMENTS 10

Article II. Judicial Notice 12
- RULE 201. JUDICIAL NOTICE OF ADJUDICATIVE FACTS 12

Article III. Presumptions in Civil Actions and Proceedings 14
- RULE 301. PRESUMPTIONS IN GENERAL IN CIVIL ACTIONS AND PROCEEDINGS 14

Article IV. Relevancy and Its Limits 15
- RULE 401. DEFINITION OF "RELEVANT EVIDENCE" 15
- RULE 402. RELEVANT EVIDENCE GENERALLY ADMISSIBLE; IRRELEVANT EVIDENCE INADMISSIBLE 15
- RULE 403. EXCLUSION OF RELEVANT EVIDENCE ON GROUNDS OF PREJUDICE, CONFUSION, OR WASTE OF TIME 15
- RULE 404. CHARACTER EVIDENCE NOT ADMISSIBLE TO PROVE CONDUCT; EXCEPTION; OTHER CRIMES 16
- RULE 405. METHODS OF PROVING CHARACTER 18
- RULE 406. HABIT; ROUTINE PRACTICE 19
- RULE 407. SUBSEQUENT REMEDIAL MEASURES 19
- RULE 408. COMPROMISE AND OFFERS TO COMPROMISE 20
- RULE 409. PAYMENT OF MEDICAL AND SIMILAR EXPENSES 21
- RULE 410. INADMISSIBILITY OF PLEAS, PLEA DISCUSSIONS, AND RELATED STATEMENTS 21
- RULE 411. LIABILITY INSURANCE 22
- RULE 412. ADMISSIBILITY OF EVIDENCE CONCERNING VICTIM'S SEXUAL CONDUCT IN CRIMINAL SEXUAL CONDUCT CASES 22

Article V. Privileges 24
RULE 501. GENERAL RULE 24
Article VI. Witnesses 25
RULE 601. COMPETENCY 25
RULE 602. LACK OF PERSONAL KNOWLEDGE 26
RULE 603. OATH OR AFFIRMATION 26
RULE 604. INTERPRETERS 27
RULE 605. COMPETENCY OF JUDGE AS WITNESS 27
RULE 606. COMPETENCY OF JUROR AS WITNESS 27
RULE 607. WHO MAY IMPEACH 29
RULE 608. EVIDENCE OF CHARACTER, CONDUCT AND BIAS OF WITNESS 29
RULE 609. IMPEACHMENT BY EVIDENCE OF CONVICTION OF CRIME 32
RULE 610. RELIGIOUS BELIEFS OR OPINIONS 35
RULE 611. MODE AND ORDER OF INTERROGATION AND PRESENTATION 35
RULE 612. WRITING USED TO REFRESH MEMORY 37
RULE 613. PRIOR STATEMENTS OF WITNESSES 38
RULE 614. CALLING AND INTERROGATION OF WITNESSES BY COURT 39
RULE 615. EXCLUSION OF WITNESSES 40
Article VII. Opinions and Expert Testimony 42
RULE 701. OPINION TESTIMONY BY LAY WITNESSES 42
RULE 702. TESTIMONY BY EXPERTS 43
RULE 703. BASES OF OPINION TESTIMONY BY EXPERTS 43
RULE 704. OPINION ON ULTIMATE ISSUE 43
RULE 705. DISCLOSURE OF FACTS OR DATA UNDERLYING EXPERT OPINION 44
Article VIII. Hearsay 45
RULE 801. DEFINITIONS 45
RULE 802. HEARSAY RULE 48
RULE 803. HEARSAY EXCEPTIONS; AVAILABILITY OF ECLARANT IMMATERIAL 48
RULE 804. HEARSAY EXCEPTIONS; DECLARANT UNAVAILABLE 58

RULE 805. HEARSAY WITHIN HEARSAY 61
RULE 806. ATTACKING AND SUPPORTING CREDIBILITY OF DECLARANT 61

Article IX. Authentication and Identification 63
RULE 901. REQUIREMENT OF AUTHENTICATION OR IDENTIFICATION 63
RULE 902. SELF-AUTHENTICATION 67
RULE 903. SUBSCRIBING WITNESS' TESTIMONY UNNECESSARY 71

Article X. Contents of Writings, Recordings, and Photographs 72
RULE 1001. DEFINITIONS 72
RULE 1002. REQUIREMENT OF ORIGINAL 73
RULE 1003. ADMISSIBILITY OF DUPLICATES 74
RULE 1004. ADMISSIBILITY OF OTHER EVIDENCE OF CONTENTS 74
RULE 1005. PUBLIC RECORDS 75
RULE 1006. SUMMARIES 75
RULE 1007. TESTIMONY OR WRITTEN ADMISSION OF PARTY 76
RULE 1008. FUNCTIONS OF COURT AND JURY 76

Article XI. Miscellaneous Rules 78
RULE 1101. APPLICABILITY OF RULES 78
RULE 1102. AMENDMENTS 80
RULE 1103. TITLE AND EFFECTIVE DATE 80

Article I. General Provisions

RULE 101. SCOPE

Except as otherwise provided by rule or by statute, these rules govern proceedings in the courts of South Carolina to the extent and with the exceptions stated in Rule 1101.

Note:

This rule differs from the federal rule in two regards. First, the phrase "except as otherwise provided by rule or by statute" is added to make it clear that statutes or other rules promulgated by the Supreme Court may limit the applicability of these rules. An example of such a rule is Rule 11 of the South Carolina Administrative and Procedural Rules for Magistrate's Court which provides that the rules of evidence apply in civil actions before the magistrate's court, but allows those rules to be relaxed in the interest of justice. Second, the phrase "courts of South Carolina" has been substituted for the phrase "courts of the United States, and before the United States bankruptcy judges and United States magistrate judges." Rule 1101 provides greater detail regarding the applicability of these rules in various proceedings.

RULE 102. PURPOSE AND CONSTRUCTION

These rules shall be construed to secure fairness in administration, elimination of unjustifiable expense and delay, and promotion of growth and development of the law of evidence to the end that the truth may be ascertained and proceedings justly determined.

Note:
This rule is identical to the federal rule.

RULE 103. RULINGS ON EVIDENCE

(a) Effect of Erroneous Ruling. Error may not be predicated upon a ruling which admits or excludes evidence unless a substantial right of the party is affected, and

(1) Objection. In case the ruling is one admitting evidence, a timely objection or motion to strike appears of record, stating the specific ground of objection, if the specific ground was not apparent from the context; or

(2) Offer of Proof. In case the ruling is one excluding evidence, the substance of the evidence and the specific evidentiary basis supporting admission were made known to the court by offer or were apparent from the context.

(b) Record of Offer and Ruling. The court may add any other or further statement which shows the character of the evidence, the form in which it was offered, the objection made, and the ruling thereon. It may direct the making of an offer in question and answer form.

(c) Hearing of Jury. In jury cases, proceedings shall be conducted, to the extent practicable, so as to prevent inadmissible evidence from being suggested to the jury by any means, such as making statements or offers of proof or asking questions in the hearing of the jury.

Note:
This rule is identical to the federal rule with the exception of the omission of subsection (d) relating to plain error. The rule of plain error contained in the federal rule is inconsistent with the law in South Carolina. Cf. State v. Torrence, 305 S.C. 45, 406 S.E.2d 315 (1991) (abolishing in favorem vitae review in capital cases and holding that error must be preserved by contemporaneous objection in the trial court). It should be noted that the Supreme Court has recognized a very few limited circumstances in which it will review issues raised for the first time on appeal. Cf. Toyota of Florence, Inc. v. Lynch, 314 S.C. 257, 442 S.E.2d 611 (1994) (challenge to abhorrent and outrageous argument raised for first time on appeal); State v. Pace, 316 S.C. 71, 447 S.E.2d 186 (1994) (failure to make contemporaneous objection to judge's comments excused where

judge's tone and tenor made it clear that any objection would have been futile). Further, the failure to adopt a rule of plain error in no way limits the authority of trial judges to raise evidentiary issues on their own motion.

Subsection (a) means that reversal on appeal is only required where a substantial right of a party has been affected; error which is harmless does not affect a substantial right. Graham, Handbook of Federal Evidence, 103.1 (3rd ed. 1981). This is equivalent to South Carolina law holding that reversal is not required unless an error is prejudicial and not harmless. State v. Sosebee, 284 S.C. 411, 326 S.E.2d 654 (1985) (probable prejudice must be shown); State v. Gaskins, 284 S.C. 105, 326 S.E.2d 132 (1985) (a new trial is not required for harmless error), cert. denied, 471 U.S. 1120, 105 S.Ct. 2368, 86 L.Ed.2d 266 (1985), overruled on other grounds, State v. Torrence, 305 S.C. 45, 406 S.E.2d 315 (1991); Watts v. Bell Oil Co., 266 S.C. 61, 221 S.E.2d 529 (1976) (prejudice must be shown).

Subsection (a)(1) is generally in accord with prior South Carolina law which required a contemporaneous objection with specific grounds to preserve an error for review. State v. Hoffman, 312 S.C. 386, 440 S.E.2d 869 (1994) (contemporaneous objection); White v. Wilbanks, 298 S.C. 225, 379 S.E.2d 298 (Ct. App.1989) (contemporaneous objection), rev'd on other grounds, 301 S.C. 560, 393 S.E.2d 182 (1990); State v. Bailey, 253 S.C. 304, 170 S.E.2d 376 (1969) (specific grounds required; general objection preserves nothing). It does somewhat relax the requirement of stating specific grounds where the grounds are apparent from the context. The better practice, however, is for counsel to always give, and the court always to require, specific grounds for an objection; this will avoid later disputes regarding what was apparent from the context. It should be noted that Rule 43(i), SCRCP, Rule 18, SCRCrimP, and Rule 9(b), SCRFC, do not prevent counsel from stating the grounds for an objection, but merely control argument on the grounds for the objection. This rule does not alter the prior practice regarding motions in limine, which allowed the motion to exclude evidence to be made at the pretrial stage, State v. Glenn, 285 S.C. 384, 330 S.E.2d 285 (1985), but required a contemporaneous objection when the evidence is actually offered into evidence at the trial to preserve the issue for review. State v. Schumpert, ___ S.C. ___, 435 S.E.2d 859 (1993); Parr v. Gaines, 309 S.C. 477, 424 S.E.2d 515 (Ct. App.1992).

Subsection (a)(2) is the federal rule modified to require the grounds for admission to be stated. As modified, this rule is consistent with South Carolina law which requires a proffer of the excluded evidence and the grounds for admission to be stated to preserve the trial court's ruling for review. State v. Cabbagestalk, 281 S.C. 35, 314 S.E.2d 10 (1984); State v. Cox, 258 S.C. 114, 187 S.E.2d 525 (1972); Legrande v. Legrande, 178 S.C. 230, 182 S.E. 432 (1935); Gold Kist, Inc. v. Citizens & Southern Nat'l Bank, 286 S.C. 272, 333 S.E.2d 67 (Ct. App.1985). The rule does change South Carolina law by dispensing with the requirement of a proffer and a statement of the grounds for admissibility where the substance of the evidence and the grounds are apparent from the context. The prior law only dispensed with the requirement of a proffer where the judge refused to allow a proffer. State v. Schmidt, 288 S.C. 301, 342 S.E.2d 401 (1986). To avoid later disputes over what was apparent from the context, however, the better practice is for a proffer and a statement of the grounds to always be made.

The first sentence of subsection (b) is similar to language contained in former Rule 43(c), SCRCP. Although no specific South Carolina case can be found to support the second sentence, requiring an offer to be made in question and answer form is within the discretion of the judge.

Subsection (c) is in accord with prior South Carolina law. Chandler v. People's Nat'l Bank, 140 S.C. 433, 138 S.E. 888 (1927); Rule 43(c), SCRCP.

RULE 104. PRELIMINARY QUESTIONS

(a) Questions of Admissibility Generally. Preliminary questions concerning the qualification of a person to be a witness, the existence of a privilege, or the admissibility of evidence shall be determined by the court, subject to the provisions of subdivision (b). In making its determination it is not bound by the rules of evidence except those with respect to privileges.

(b) Relevancy Conditioned on Fact. When the relevancy of evidence depends upon the fulfillment of a condition of fact, the court shall admit it upon, or subject to, the introduction of evidence sufficient to support a finding of the fulfillment of the condition.

(c) Hearing of Jury. Hearings on the admissibility of confessions or statements by an accused, and pretrial identifications of an accused shall in all cases be conducted out of the hearing of the jury. Hearings on other preliminary matters shall be so conducted when the interests of justice require, or when an accused is a witness and so requests.

(d) Testimony by Accused. The accused does not, by testifying upon a preliminary matter, become subject to cross-examination as to other issues in the case.

(e) Weight and Credibility. This rule does not limit the right of a party to introduce before the jury evidence relevant to weight or credibility.

Note:
Except for subsection (c), this rule is identical to the federal rule.

The first sentence of subsection (a) is in accord with prior South Carolina law. Wright v. Pub. Sav. Life Ins. Co., 262 S.C. 285, 204 S.E.2d 57 (1974). No South Carolina authority has been found which specifically determines whether a judge must apply the rules of evidence in conducting a hearing on the admissibility of evidence. Cf. Congdon v. Morgan, 14 S.C. 587 (1880) (passing comment that judge did not violate rules of evidence during hearing on admissibility of evidence).

Subsection (b) addresses situations where the relevancy of an item of evidence depends upon the existence of a particular preliminary fact. Prior South Carolina case law has recognized that a judge commits no error in admitting evidence where its relevancy is established later in the trial. Perry v. Jefferies, 61 S.C. 292, 39 S.E. 515 (1901) (evidence of acts of defendant's agents admitted before any evidence of agency introduced).

Subsection (c) modifies the federal rule by adding the phrase "or statements made by an accused, and pretrial identifications of an accused." This addition is made to emphasize the fact that hearings on the admissibility of all statements made by a criminal defendant, whether inculpatory or exculpatory, must be made outside the presence of the jury. State v. Primus, 312 S.C. 256, 440 S.E.2d 128 (1994); State v. Lee, 255 S.C. 309, 178 S.E.2d 652 (1971). The addition also requires all hearings regarding the admissibility of pretrial identifications (to include any assertion that an in-court identification should be excluded as a result of a pretrial identification) to be heard outside the presence of the jury. State v. Simmons, 308 S.C. 80, 417 S.E.2d 92 (1992).

No South Carolina cases have been found which address the matters stated in subsections (d) and (e).

RULE 105. LIMITED ADMISSIBILITY

When evidence which is admissible as to one party or for one purpose but not admissible as to another party or for another purpose is admitted, the court, upon request, shall restrict the evidence to its proper scope and instruct the jury accordingly.

Note:
This rule is identical to the federal rule and is in accord with prior South Carolina law. State v. Bottoms, 260 S.C. 187, 195 S.E.2d 116 (1973); State v. Bagwell, 201 S.C. 387, 23 S.E.2d 244 (1942).

RULE 106. REMAINDER OF OR RELATED WRITINGS OR STATEMENTS

When a writing, or recorded statement, or part thereof is introduced by a party, an adverse party may require the introduction at that time of any other part or any other writing or recorded statement which ought in fairness to be considered contemporaneously with it.

Note:
The law in this State has been that, when a part of a document or writing is introduced into evidence, the remainder may be introduced by the other party. Dukes v. Smoak, 181 S.C. 182, 186 S.E. 780 (1936). The same rule was applicable to conversations. State v. Jackson, 265 S.C. 278, 217 S.E.2d 794 (1975). However, the party seeking to bring out the remainder had to wait until cross-examination or the presentation of that party's case to do so. This rule, which is identical to the federal rule, changes the prior law as to written or recorded statements. The party seeking to introduce the remainder of a written or recorded statement can now require the remainder to be introduced at the same time the other part of the written or recorded statement is introduced. This rule does not change the order of proof as to the remainder of an unrecorded conversation; the party seeking to bring out the remainder must do so during cross-examination or during that party's case.

Article II. Judicial Notice

RULE 201. JUDICIAL NOTICE OF ADJUDICATIVE FACTS

(a) Scope of Rule. This rule governs only judicial notice of adjudicative facts.

(b) Kinds of Facts. A judicially noticed fact must be one not subject to reasonable dispute in that it is either (1) generally known within the territorial jurisdiction of the trial court or (2) capable of accurate and ready determination by resort to sources whose accuracy cannot reasonably be questioned.

(c) When Discretionary. A court may take judicial notice, whether requested or not.

(d) When Mandatory. A court shall take judicial notice if requested by a party and supplied with the necessary information.

(e) Opportunity to Be Heard. A party is entitled upon timely request to an opportunity to be heard as to the propriety of taking judicial notice and the tenor of the matter noticed. In the absence of prior notification, the request may be made after judicial notice has been taken.

(f) Time of Taking Notice. Judicial notice may be taken at any stage of the proceeding.

(g) Instructing Jury. The court shall instruct the jury to accept as conclusive any fact judicially noticed.

Note:
Except for subsection (g), this rule is identical to the federal rule. As stated by subsection (a), this rule governs only judicial notice of adjudicative facts. Adjudicative facts are "facts about the particular event which gave rise to the lawsuit and ... [help] explain who did what, when, where, how and with what motive and intent." Legislative facts, on the other hand, are the factual grounds on which judges base their opinions "when deciding

upon the constitutional validity of a statute, interpreting a statute, or extending or restricting a common law rule." C. McCormick, McCormick on Evidence 328 and 331 (4th ed. 1992). The courts of this State continue to have authority to take judicial notice of legislative facts. Cf. Davenport v. City of Rock Hill, 315 S.C. 114, 432 S.E.2d 451 (1993) (history of tax anticipation notes considered).

Subsection (b) is consistent with prior case law in this State. See In Re Harry C., 280 S.C. 308, 313 S.E.2d 287 (1984); State v. Broad River Power Co., 177 S.C. 240, 181 S.E. 41 (1935). This rule does not allow a judge to take judicial notice of a fact merely because it is within his personal knowledge, and the case of Gamble v. Price, 289 S.C. 538, 347 S.E.2d 131 (Ct. App.1986) is inconsistent with this rule.

Regarding subsection (c), no South Carolina case has been found discussing this matter.

Subsection (d) is consistent with prior case law in this State. See Toole v. Salter, 249 S.C. 354, 154 S.E.2d 434 (1967); State v. Broad River Power Co., 177 S.C. 240, 181 S.E. 41 (1935).

Regarding subsection (e), the law of this State has not previously entitled a party to be heard on the issue of taking judicial notice. This opportunity appears to be a useful safeguard to protect a party's rights. J. Weinstein and M. Berger, Weinstein's Evidence, 201[05] (1994).

Subsection (f) is consistent with prior case law in this State. Cf . State v. Squires, 311 S.C. 11, 426 S.E.2d 738 (1992) (Supreme Court took judicial notice that infrared spectroscopy process had gained general acceptance in the scientific community); McCoy v. Town of York, 193 S.C. 390, 8 S.E.2d 905 (1940) (Supreme Court took judicial notice of dangerous qualities of gasoline and kerosene).

Subsection (g) requires a court to instruct the jury to accept as conclusive any fact judicially noticed. The rule differs from the federal rule in that it makes no distinction between civil and criminal cases. The language of the rule is taken from the 1974 Uniform Rules of Evidence, Rule 201.

Article III. Presumptions in Civil Actions and Proceedings

RULE 301. PRESUMPTIONS IN GENERAL IN CIVIL ACTIONS AND PROCEEDINGS

In all civil actions and proceedings not otherwise provided for by statute or by these rules, a presumption imposes on the party against whom it is directed the burden of going forward with evidence to rebut or meet the presumption, but does not shift to such party the burden of proof in the sense of the risk of nonperfusion, which remains throughout the trial upon the party on whom it was originally cast.

Note:

This rule is the same as the federal rule. It is consistent with the case law in this State. See Long v. Metropolitan Life Insurance Co., 228 S.C. 498, 90 S.E.2d 915 (1956); Ford v. Atlantic Coast Line R. Co., 169 S.C. 41, 168 S.E. 143 (1932).

Article IV. Relevancy and Its Limits

RULE 401. DEFINITION OF "RELEVANT EVIDENCE"

"Relevant evidence" means evidence having any tendency to make the existence of any fact that is of consequence to the determination of the action more probable or less probable than it would be without the evidence.

Note:

This rule is identical to the federal rule and is consistent with South Carolina law. State v. Alexander, 303 S.C. 377, 401 S.E.2d 146 (1991); State v. Schmidt, 288 S.C. 301, 342 S.E.2d 401 (1986).

RULE 402. RELEVANT EVIDENCE GENERALLY ADMISSIBLE; IRRELEVANT EVIDENCE INADMISSIBLE

All relevant evidence is admissible, except as otherwise provided by the Constitution of the United States, the Constitution of the State of South Carolina, statutes, these rules, or by other rules promulgated by the Supreme Court of South Carolina. Evidence which is not relevant is not admissible.

Note:

This rule is the federal rule amended to reference South Carolina law. The rule reflects the law in South Carolina. Levy v. Outdoor Resorts of South Carolina, 304 S.C. 427, 405 S.E.2d 387 (1991); State v. Petit, 144 S.C. 452, 142 S.E. 725 (1928).

RULE 403. EXCLUSION OF RELEVANT EVIDENCE ON GROUNDS OF PREJUDICE, CONFUSION, OR WASTE OF TIME

Although relevant, evidence may be excluded if its probative value is substantially outweighed by the danger of unfair prejudice, confusion of the issues, or misleading the jury, or by considerations of undue delay, waste of time, or needless presentation of cumulative evidence.

Note:

This rule is identical to the federal rule and is consistent with the law in South Carolina. State v. Alexander, 303 S.C. 377, 401 S.E.2d 146 (1991) (relevant evidence may be excluded where its probative value is substantially outweighed by the danger of unfair prejudice); State v. Hess, 279 S.C. 14, 301 S.E.2d 547 (limitation of defense testimony upheld where it was merely cumulative to other testimony), cert. denied, 464 U.S. 827, 104 S.Ct. 100, 78 L.Ed.2d 105 (1983); State v. Gregory, 198 S.C. 98, 16 S.E.2d 532 (1941) (trial judge properly limited the defendant's presentation of certain evidence to guard against confusion of the jury by the injection of collateral issues).

RULE 404. CHARACTER EVIDENCE NOT ADMISSIBLE TO PROVE CONDUCT; EXCEPTION; OTHER CRIMES

(a) Character Evidence Generally. Evidence of a person's character or a trait of character is not admissible for the purpose of proving action in conformity therewith on a particular occasion, except:

(1) Character of Accused. Evidence of a pertinent trait of character offered by an accused, or by the prosecution to rebut the same;

(2) Character of Victim. Evidence of a pertinent trait of character of the victim of the crime offered by an accused, or by the prosecution to rebut the same, or evidence of a character trait of peacefulness of the victim offered by the prosecution in a homicide case to rebut evidence that the victim was the first aggressor;

(3) Character of Witness. Evidence of the character of a witness, as provided in Rules 607, 608, and 609.

(b) Other Crimes, Wrongs, or Acts. Evidence of other crimes, wrongs, or acts is not admissible to prove the character of a person in order to show action in conformity therewith. It may, however, be admissible to show motive, identity, the existence of a common scheme or plan, the absence of mistake or accident, or intent.

Note:

Rule 404(a) is identical to the federal rule and is consistent with the law in South Carolina. State v. Peake, 302 S.C. 378, 396 S.E.2d 362 (1990).

Rule 404(a)(1) is identical to the federal rule and is consistent with the law in South Carolina. State v. Lyles, 210 S.C. 87, 41 S.E.2d 625 (1947) (a defendant may put in evidence of his good character); State v. Major, 301 S.C. 181, 391 S.E.2d 235 (1990) (when the accused offers evidence of his good character regarding specific character traits relevant to the crime charged, the state may cross-examine as to acts relating to the traits focused on by the accused).

Rule 404(a)(2) identical to the federal rule and is consistent with the law in South Carolina. State v. Boyd, 126 S.C. 300, 119 S.E. 839 (1923).

Rule 404(b) differs in two respects from the federal rule. First, unlike the federal rule which does not limit the purposes for which evidence of other crimes may be admitted, the South Carolina rule limits the use of evidence of other crimes, wrongs, or acts to those enumerated in State v. Lyle, 125 S.C. 406, 118 S.E. 803 (1923). See also Citizens Bank of Darlington v. McDonald, 202 S.C. 244, 24 S.E.2d 369 (1943) (Lyle applicable in civil cases). Second, the South Carolina rule does not contain the requirement which is in the federal rule that, upon request by an accused, the prosecution must provide reasonable notice of the general nature of any evidence it intends to introduce under the rule. With the exception of notice of evidence to be used in aggravation in the sentencing phase of capital cases, S.C. Code Ann. § 16-3-20(B) (Supp. 1993), there is no similar requirement under South Carolina law. The rule does not set forth the burden of proof required for the admission of evidence of bad acts not the subject of a conviction and, therefore, case law would control. State v. Smith, 300 S.C. 216, 387 S.E.2d 245 (1989) (in a criminal case, evidence of other crimes or bad acts must be clear and convincing if the acts are not the subject of a conviction). Further, when the prejudicial effect of evidence substantially outweighs its probative value, the evidence may be excluded under Rule 403 which is consistent with prior case law. State v. Garner, 304 S.C. 220, 403 S.E.2d 631 (1991).

RULE 405. METHODS OF PROVING CHARACTER

(a) Reputation or Opinion. In all cases in which evidence of character or a trait of character of a person is admissible, proof may be made by testimony as to reputation or by testimony in the form of an opinion. On cross-examination, inquiry is allowable into relevant specific instances of conduct.

(b) Specific Instances of Conduct. In cases in which character or a trait of character of a person is an essential element of a charge, claim, or defense, proof may also be made of specific instances of that person's conduct.

Note:

Rule 405(a) is identical to the federal rule and changes the law in South Carolina in one respect. Formerly, only testimony as to a person's general reputation was allowed. State v. Groome, 274 S.C. 189, 262 S.E.2d 31 (1980); In re Greenfield's Estate, 245 S.C. 595, 141 S.E.2d 916 (1965). Rule 405(a) allows evidence of character to be in the form of opinion or reputation evidence. The portion of Rule 405(a) regarding cross-examination as to specific acts is consistent with the law in South Carolina. State v. Major, 301 S.C. 181, 391 S.E.2d 235 (1990) (when the accused offers evidence of his good character regarding specific character traits relevant to the crime charged, the state may cross-examine as to particular bad acts or conduct relating to the traits focused on by the accused).

Rule 405(b) is identical to the federal rule and is consistent with South Carolina law. State v. Amburgey, 206 S.C. 426, 34 S.E.2d 779 (1945).

RULE 406. HABIT; ROUTINE PRACTICE

Evidence of the habit of a person or of the routine practice of an organization, whether corroborated or not and regardless of the presence of eyewitnesses, is relevant to prove that the conduct of the person or organization on a particular occasion was in conformity with the habit or routine practice.

Note:

This rule is identical to the federal rule and makes it clear that the presence or absence of eyewitnesses does not affect the relevancy of evidence of habit or routine practice. To the extent that South Carolina law regarding evidence of habit or routine was previously read to require the absence of eyewitnesses, this rule constitutes a change in the law. Compare Laney v. Atlantic Coast Line Railway Co., 211 S.C. 328, 45 S.E.2d 184 (1947); State v. Hester, 137 S.C. 145, 134 S.E. 885 (1926); Dowling v. Fenner, 131 S.C. 62, 126 S.E. 432 (1922) with Holcombe v. Watson Supply Co., 171 S.C. 110, 171 S.E. 604 (1933).

RULE 407. SUBSEQUENT REMEDIAL MEASURES

When, after an event, measures are taken which, if taken previously, would have made the event less likely to occur, evidence of the subsequent measures is not admissible to prove negligence or culpable conduct in connection with the event. This rule does not require the exclusion of evidence of subsequent measures when offered for another purpose, such as proving ownership, control, or feasibility of precautionary measures, if controverted, or impeachment.

Note:

This rule is identical to the federal rule. The general rule that evidence of subsequent measures is inadmissible to establish negligence is consistent with South Carolina law. Green v. Atlantic Coast Line R. Co., 136 S.C. 337, 134 S.E. 385 (1926). Under South Carolina law another stated purpose for admitting evidence of subsequent measures is to show the conditions existing at the time of the event or accident. Taylor v. Nix,

307 S.C. 551, 416 S.E.2d 619 (1992); Plunkett v. Clearwater Bleachery Mfg. Co., 80 S.C. 310, 61 S.E. 431 (1906); see also Eargle v. Sumter Lighting Co., 110 S.C. 560, 96 S.E. 909 (1918).

RULE 408. COMPROMISE AND OFFERS TO COMPROMISE

Evidence of (1) furnishing or offering or promising to furnish, or (2) accepting or offering or promising to accept, a valuable consideration in compromising or attempting to compromise a claim which was disputed as to either validity or amount, is not admissible to prove liability for or invalidity of the claim or its amount. Evidence of conduct or statements made in compromise negotiations is likewise not admissible. This rule does not require the exclusion of any evidence otherwise discoverable merely because it is presented in the course of compromise negotiations. This rule also does not require exclusion when the evidence is offered for another purpose, such as proving bias or prejudice of a witness, negativing a contention of undue delay, or proving an effort to obstruct a criminal investigation or prosecution.

Note:

This rule is identical to the federal rule. It is generally the rule in South Carolina that evidence relating to settlements is not admissible to prove liability. Hunter v. Hyder, 236 S.C. 378, 114 S.E.2d 493 (1960); see also Woodward v. Southern Railway, 88 S.C. 453, 70 S.E. 1060 (1911) (evidence of disclosures made by either party to the other, directly or indirectly, in negotiations for a compromise is not admissible). Evidence of an offer to compromise may be admissible for some other purpose. Meehan v. Commercial Casualty Ins. Co., 166 S.C. 496, 165 S.E. 194 (1932) (evidence of offers of compromise made by alleged agent of a party admissible for purpose of proving agency).

RULE 409. PAYMENT OF MEDICAL AND SIMILAR EXPENSES

Evidence of furnishing or offering or promising to pay medical, hospital, or similar expenses occasioned by an injury is not admissible to prove liability for the injury.

Note:

This rule is identical to the federal rule. Formerly, South Carolina law, while generally prohibiting the admission of evidence of offers to pay, or payment of, medical or other expenses, McIntire v. Winn Dixie Greenville, Inc., 275 S.C. 323, 270 S.E.2d 440 (1980), did allow its admission if the circumstances surrounding the payment indicated an admission of liability rather than an act of benevolence. Crosby v. Southeast Zayre, Inc., 274 S.C. 519, 265 S.E.2d 517 (1980). The rule strictly prohibits the admission of evidence of offers to pay, or payment of, medical or other similar expenses.

RULE 410. INADMISSIBILITY OF PLEAS, PLEA DISCUSSIONS, AND RELATED STATEMENTS

Except as otherwise provided in this rule, evidence of the following is not, in any civil or criminal proceeding, admissible against the defendant who made the plea or was a participant in the plea discussions:

(1) a plea of guilty which was later withdrawn;

(2) a plea of nolo contendere;

(3) any statement made in the course of any court proceedings regarding either of the foregoing pleas; or

(4) any statement made in the course of plea discussions with an attorney for the prosecuting authority which do not result in a plea of guilty or which result in a plea of guilty later withdrawn.

However, such a statement is admissible (i) in any proceeding wherein another statement made in the course of the same plea or plea discussions has been introduced and the statement ought in fairness be considered contemporaneously with it, or (ii) in a criminal proceeding for perjury or false statement if the statement was made by the defendant under oath, on the record and in the presence of counsel.

Note:

Except for subsection (3), this rule is identical to the federal rule. Subsection (3) was amended because South Carolina has no equivalent to Rule 11 of the Federal Rules of Criminal Procedure. It should be noted that convictions based on pleas of nolo contendere are admissible under Rule 609 for impeachment. The rule is consistent with prior South Carolina law. State v. Mathis, 287 S.C. 589, 340 S.E.2d 538 (1986); State v. Lynn, 277 S.C. 222, 284 S.E.2d 786 (1981).

RULE 411. LIABILITY INSURANCE

Evidence that a person was or was not insured against liability is not admissible upon the issue whether the person acted negligently or otherwise wrongfully. This rule does not require the exclusion of evidence of insurance against liability when offered for another purpose, such as proof of agency, ownership, or control, or bias or prejudice of a witness.

Note:

This rule is identical to the federal rule and is consistent with the law in South Carolina. Dunn v. Charleston Coca-Cola Bottling Co., 311 S.C. 43, 426 S.E.2d 756 (1993) (the fact that a defendant is protected from liability by insurance shall not be made known to the jury); Sarvis v. Register, 288 S.C. 236, 341 S.E.2d 791 (1986) (generally, the existence of insurance should not be brought to the attention of the jury).

RULE 412. ADMISSIBILITY OF EVIDENCE CONCERNING VICTIM'S SEXUAL CONDUCT IN CRIMINAL SEXUAL CONDUCT CASES

In prosecutions for criminal sexual conduct or assault with intent to commit criminal sexual conduct, the admissibility of evidence concerning the victim's sexual conduct is subject to the limitations contained in S.C. Code Ann. 16-3-659.1 (1985).

Note:

In a prosecution for criminal sexual conduct or assault with intent to commit criminal sexual conduct, the admissibility of evidence of the victim's sexual conduct is controlled by S.C. Code Ann. 16-3-659.1 (1985). Unlike the federal rule which contains the standards and procedures governing the admissibility of such evidence, this rule merely references the statute.

Article V. Privileges

RULE 501. GENERAL RULE

Except as required by the Constitution of South Carolina, by the Constitution of the United States or by South Carolina statute, the privilege of a witness, person or government shall be governed by the principles of the common law as they may be interpreted by the courts in the light of reason and experience.

Note:

This rule modifies the federal rule to refer to the South Carolina Constitution and statutes. Like the federal rule, this rule does not set forth a list of privileges. Among those privileges which would be covered by this rule are: husband and wife (S.C. Code Ann. 19-11-30); priest and penitent (S.C. Code Ann. 19-11-90); certain mental health professionals and clients (S.C. Code Ann. 19-11-95); news media and sources (S.C. Code Ann. 19-11-100); attorney and client [Drayton v. Industrial Life & Health Ins. Co., 205 S.C. 98, 31 S.E.2d 148 (1944)]; privilege against self-incrimination (U.S. Const. amend. V; S.C. Const. art. I, 12; S.C. Code Ann. 19-11-80); and the identity of a confidential informant [State v. Hayward, 302 S.C. 75, 393 S.E.2d 918 (1990)].

Article VI. Witnesses

RULE 601. COMPETENCY

(a) General Rule. Every person is competent to be a witness except as otherwise provided by statute or these rules.

(b) Disqualification of a Witness. A person is disqualified to be a witness if the court determines that (1) the proposed witness is incapable of expressing himself concerning the matter as to be understood by the judge and jury either directly or through interpretation by one who can understand him, or (2) the proposed witness is incapable of understanding the duty of a witness to tell the truth.

Note:

Subsection (a) differs from the federal rule which provides that the only exceptions to the competency rule are those set forth in the Rules of Evidence. Because legislation such as the Dead Man's Statute, S.C. Code Ann. § 19-11-20 (1985), still exists limiting witness competency, the rule also refers to exceptions provided by statute.

At common law, there were numerous grounds which would render a witness incompetent. Legislation has eliminated many of these common law disqualifications resulting in a liberalization of the rules regarding competency. See, e.g., S.C. Code Ann. §§ 19-11-10 (1985) (party competent to be witness); 19-11-30 (Supp. 1993) (spouse of party competent); 19-11-40 (1985) (witness having interest in action is not disqualified); 19-11-50 (1985) (criminal defendant may testify); 19-11-60 (1985) (convicted person may testify). Subsection (a) continues this trend of liberalization by creating a general rule of competency.

This rule will result in a change in the law regarding competency of children. Under prior South Carolina law, proof of competency for children under the age of fourteen was required unless the child was a victim of abuse or neglect, as defined in the Children's Code, who was testifying concerning the abuse or neglect. South Carolina Department of Social Services v. Doe, 292 S.C. 211, 355 S.E.2d 543 (Ct. App.1987); S.C. Code Ann. § 19-11-25 (Supp. 1993). Under this rule, children are presumed to be competent unless it is shown otherwise.

The federal rule does not contain a subsection (b). This provision was added to establish a minimum standard for competency of a witness and to make it clear that the determination of a witness' competency is within the sound discretion of the trial judge. In re Robert M., 294 S.C. 69, 362 S.E.2d 639 (1987); State v. Camele, 293 S.C. 302, 360 S.E.2d 307 (1987); State v. Pitts, 256 S.C. 420, 182 S.E.2d 738 (1971).

RULE 602. LACK OF PERSONAL KNOWLEDGE

A witness may not testify to a matter unless evidence is introduced sufficient to support a finding that the witness has personal knowledge of the matter. Evidence to prove personal knowledge may, but need not, consist of the witness' own testimony. This rule is subject to the provisions of Rule 703, relating to opinion testimony by expert witnesses.

Note:

This rule is identical to the federal rule and is consistent with South Carolina law. See Gentry v. Watkins-Carolina Trucking Co., 249 S.C. 316, 154 S.E.2d 112 (1967); Wilson v. Clary, 212 S.C. 250, 47 S.E.2d 618 (1948).

RULE 603. OATH OR AFFIRMATION

Before testifying, every witness shall be required to declare that the witness will testify truthfully, by oath or affirmation administered in a form calculated to awaken the witness' conscience and impress the witness' mind with the duty to do so.

Note:

This rule is identical to the federal rule which sets forth the common law tenet that a witness is required to take an oath or affirmation to tell the truth before being allowed to testify. See 98 C.J.S. Witnesses § 320(a) (1957). The use of an affirmation instead of an oath is consistent with prior law. See S.C. Code Ann. § 19-1-40 (1985); Rule 43(d), SCRCP.

RULE 604. INTERPRETERS

An interpreter is subject to the provisions of these rules relating to qualification as an expert and the administration of an oath or affirmation to make a true translation.

Note:
This rule is identical to the federal rule. The qualification of an interpreter is within the discretion of the trial judge and depends on the circumstances of each case. Peoples National Bank v. Manos Brothers, 226 S.C. 257, 84 S.E.2d 857 (1954).

RULE 605. COMPETENCY OF JUDGE AS WITNESS

The judge presiding at the trial may not testify in that trial as a witness.

Note:
This rule is identical to the first sentence of the federal rule and is consistent with South Carolina law providing that a judge may not testify as a witness in a case being tried before that judge. State v. Bagwell, 201 S.C. 387, 23 S.E.2d 244 (1942). The second sentence of the federal rule dispenses with the requirement of an objection to a judge being a witness. This sentence was deleted as being inconsistent with the law of this state. See State v. Torrence, 305 S.C. 45, 406 S.E.2d 315 (1991).

RULE 606. COMPETENCY OF JUROR AS WITNESS

(a) At the Trial. A member of the jury may not testify as a witness before that jury in the trial of the case in which the juror is sitting. If the juror is called so to testify, the opposing party shall be afforded an opportunity to object outside the presence of the jury.

(b) Inquiry Into Validity of Verdict or Indictment. Upon an inquiry into the validity of a verdict or indictment, a juror may not testify as to any matter or statement occurring during the course of the jury's deliberations or to the effect of anything upon that or any other juror's mind or emotions as influencing the juror to assent to or dissent from the verdict or indictment or concerning the juror's mental processes in connection therewith, except that a juror may testify on the question whether extraneous prejudicial information was improperly brought to the jury's attention or whether any outside influence was improperly brought to bear upon any juror. Nor may a juror's affidavit or evidence of any statement by the juror concerning a matter about which the juror would be precluded from testifying be received for these purposes.

Note:

The language of this rule is identical to the federal rule. Subsection (a) of this rule changes the law in South Carolina in two regards. First, while prior law allowed a juror to testify as to venue, State v. Vari, 35 S.C. 175, 14 S.E. 392 (1892) (juror allowed to testify as to isolated, particular matter such as value or venue but not as to general facts and circumstances of the offense), this subsection would prohibit such testimony. Second, the prior law did not require that the party opposing the calling of a juror as a witness be given an opportunity to object outside the presence of the jury.

Subsection (b) is consistent with the general rule that a juror may not present testimony as to the deliberations in the jury room; as to any mistake, irregularity, or misconduct on the part of the jurors; or which would impeach the verdict or contradict the record. Barsh v. Chrysler Corp., 262 S.C. 129, 203 S.E.2d 107 (1974); State v. Wells, 249 S.C. 249, 153 S.E.2d 904 (1967); Caines v. Marion Coca-Cola Bottling Co., 196 S.C. 502, 14 S.E.2d 10 (1941). An affidavit of a juror has been admitted on a post-trial motion "with great hesitation" when there was an allegation that a party had attempted to influence the juror. Cohen v. Robert, 33 S.C.L. (2 Strob.) 410 (1848). The rule is also consistent with

South Carolina cases holding that no one may invade the secrecy of a grand jury's deliberations. State v. Sanders, 251 S.C. 431, 163 S.E.2d 220 (1968); Margolis v. Telech, 239 S.C. 232, 122 S.E.2d 417 (1961).

RULE 607. WHO MAY IMPEACH

The credibility of a witness may be attacked by any party, including the party calling the witness.

Note:

This rule is identical to the federal rule. However, it is contrary to the former law in this State that a party must vouch for its own witness and may not impeach its witness unless the witness is declared hostile upon a showing of actual surprise and harm, or unless the party is required to call someone, such as a subscribing witness to a deed or will, as a witness. State v. Anderson, 304 S.C. 551, 406 S.E.2d 152 (1991); Hicks v. Coleman, 240 S.C. 227, 125 S.E.2d 473 (1962); White v. Southern Oil Stores, Inc., 198 S.C. 173, 17 S.E.2d 150 (1941).

RULE 608. EVIDENCE OF CHARACTER, CONDUCT AND BIAS OF WITNESS

(a) Opinion and Reputation Evidence of Character. The credibility of a witness may be attacked or supported by evidence in the form of opinion or reputation, but subject to these limitations: (1) the evidence may refer only to character for truthfulness or untruthfulness, and (2) evidence of truthful character is admissible only after the character of the witness for truthfulness has been attacked by opinion or reputation evidence or otherwise.

(b) Specific Instances of Conduct. Specific instances of the conduct of a witness, for the purpose of attacking or supporting the witness' credibility, other than conviction of crime as provided in Rule 609, may not be proved by extrinsic evidence. They may, however, in the discretion of the court, if probative of truthfulness or untruthfulness, be inquired into on cross-examination of the witness (1) concerning the witness' character for truthfulness or untruthfulness, or (2) concerning the character for truthfulness or untruthfulness of another witness as to which character the witness being cross-examined has testified.

The giving of testimony, whether by an accused or by any other witness, does not operate as a waiver of the accused's or the witness' privilege against self-incrimination when examined with respect to matters which relate only to credibility.

(c) Evidence of Bias. Bias, prejudice or any motive to misrepresent may be shown to impeach the witness either by examination of the witness or by evidence otherwise adduced.

Note:
Except for the addition of subsection (c), this rule is identical to the federal rule.

Subsection (a) of this rule permits a witness' truthfulness to be impeached by opinion or reputation evidence. The general rule in South Carolina is that a witness' general reputation for truth and veracity is placed in issue when taking the witness stand. See State v. Major, 301 S.C. 181, 391 S.E.2d 235 (1990); State v. Robertson, 26 S.C. 117, 1 S.E. 443 (1887); State v. Hale, 284 S.C. 348, 326 S.E.2d 418 (Ct. App.1985), cert. denied, 286 S.C. 127, 332 S.E.2d 533 1985). Formerly, although evidence of a person's general reputation in the community was admissible, opinion testimony was not admissible. State v. Groome, 274 S.C. 189, 262 S.E.2d 31 (1980); In re: Greenfield's Estate, 245 S.C. 595, 141 S.E.2d 916 (1965). The provision prohibiting bolstering of a witness until after the witness' credibility is attacked is consistent with prior South Carolina law. State v. Lynn, 277 S.C. 222, 284 S.E.2d 786 (1981); Woods v. Thrower, 116 S.C. 165, 107 S.E. 250 (1921). However, there was an exception allowing bolstering prior to attack when the witness was a stranger to the community. State v. Lynn, supra; Woods v. Thrower, supra. This exception is not included in the rule.

As to subsection (b), no South Carolina cases have been found which permit cross-examination regarding specific acts to show truthfulness.

The use of specific acts to attack credibility is similar to prior South Carolina case law which allowed a witness to be cross-examined about prior bad acts if they constituted crimes of moral turpitude. State v. Outlaw, 307 S.C. 177, 414 S.E.2d 147 (1992); State v. Major, 301 S.C. 181, 391 S.E.2d 235 (1990); State v. McGuire, 272 S.C. 547, 253 S.E.2d 103 (1979). The cross-examiner was required to take the answer given by the witness and could not use extrinsic evidence or other testimony to prove the bad act. State v. Outlaw, supra; State v. Major, supra. Additionally, the inquiry could only go so far as to bring out the general nature of the misconduct and could not go into specific details. State v. Outlaw, supra; State v. Major, supra.

Subsection (b), like its federal counterpart, does not set forth what conduct may adversely affect a witness' credibility. The former case law standard, which allowed impeachment if the conduct was a crime of moral turpitude, is not the appropriate standard in light of the Court's decision to abandon the moral turpitude standard under Rule 609. Instead, the trial courts should be guided by the decisions of the federal courts which limit inquiry into those specific instances of misconduct which are "clearly probative of truthfulness or untruthfulness" such as forgery, bribery, false pretenses, and embezzlement. See Weinstein's Evidence, 608[05] (1994). This will reduce the kinds of misconduct which can be inquired into from that permitted under prior law. Further, this rule, like the prior case law, does not allow a cross-examiner to go on a "fishing expedition" in the hopes of finding some misconduct. State v. McGuire, supra. The decision whether to allow such impeachment remains in the discretion of the trial judge. Id.

Subsection (c) was added to address impeachment by showing bias or impartiality. State v. Brewington, 267 S.C. 97, 226 S.E.2d 249 (1976); North Greenville College v. Sherman Const. Co., Inc., 270 S.C. 553, 243 S.E.2d 441 (1978).

RULE 609. IMPEACHMENT BY EVIDENCE OF CONVICTION OF CRIME

(a) General Rule. For the purpose of attacking the credibility of a witness,

(1) evidence that a witness other than an accused has been convicted of a crime shall be admitted, subject to Rule 403, if the crime was punishable by death or imprisonment in excess of one year under the law under which the witness was convicted, and evidence that an accused has been convicted of such a crime shall be admitted if the court determines that the probative value of admitting this evidence outweighs its prejudicial effect to the accused; and

(2) evidence that any witness has been convicted of a crime shall be admitted if it involved dishonesty or false statement, regardless of the punishment.

For the purposes of this rule, a conviction includes a conviction resulting from a trial or any type of plea, including a plea of nolo contendere or a plea pursuant to North Carolina v. Alford, 400 U.S. 25 (1970).

(b) Time Limit. Evidence of a conviction under this rule is not admissible if a period of more than ten years has elapsed since the date of the conviction or of the release of the witness from the confinement imposed for that conviction, whichever is the later date, unless the court determines, in the interests of justice, that the probative value of the conviction supported by specific facts and circumstances substantially outweighs its prejudicial effect. However, evidence of a conviction more than 10 years old as calculated herein, is not admissible unless the proponent gives to the adverse party sufficient advance written notice of intent to use such evidence to provide the adverse party with a fair opportunity to contest the use of such evidence.

(c) Effect of Pardon, Annulment, or Certificate of Rehabilitation or Other Equivalent Procedure. Evidence of a conviction is not admissible under this rule if (1) the conviction has been the subject of a pardon, annulment, certificate of rehabilitation, or other equivalent procedure based on a finding of the rehabilitation of the person convicted, and that person has not been convicted of a subsequent crime which was punishable by death or imprisonment in excess of one year, or (2) the conviction has been the subject of a pardon, annulment, or other equivalent procedure based on a finding of innocence.

(d) Juvenile Adjudications. Evidence of a juvenile adjudication is admissible under this rule if conviction of the crime would be admissible to attack the credibility of an adult.

(e) Pendency of Appeal. The pendency of an appeal therefrom does not render evidence of a conviction inadmissible. Evidence of the pendency of an appeal is admissible.

Note:
Except for subsections (a) and (d), this rule is identical to the federal rule.

Subsection (a) is identical to the federal rule except for the addition of the last sentence. This addition was made to make it clear that the term "conviction" includes a conviction resulting from a trial or any type of plea, to include a plea of nolo contendere or a plea pursuant to North Carolina v. Alford, 400 U.S. 25, 91 S.Ct. 160, 27 L.Ed.2d 162 (1970). Allowing a plea of nolo contendere to be used for impeachment is consistent with the prior law. State v. Lynn, 277 S.C. 222, 284 S.E.2d 786 (1981). Subsection (a) does change the law in South Carolina. The prior law was that a witness could be impeached by evidence that the witness had been convicted of a crime of moral turpitude. State v. Hale, 284 S.C. 348, 326 S.E.2d 418 (Ct.App.1985), cert. denied, 286 S.C. 127, 332 S.E.2d 533 (1985); State v. Harvey, 275 S.C. 225, 268 S.E.2d 587 (1980). Further, the standard for balancing probative value against prejudicial effect was the same for all witnesses, to include the accused in a criminal case. Green v. Hewett, 305 S.C. 238, 407 S.E.2d 651 (1991). This subsection does not use the moral turpitude standard, but instead allows impeachment with a conviction for any crime which carries a maximum sentence of death or imprisonment for more than one year. Further, the rule provides for a different standard for balancing probative value and prejudicial effect for an accused who is a witness.

Regarding subsection (b), the adoption of a general ten year limit on the use of convictions for impeachment constitutes a change in South Carolina law. The former case law did not set forth a time limit on the use of convictions for impeachment. Green v. Hewett, supra. Instead, the determination whether a conviction was too remote rested in the discretion of the trial judge. Horton v. State, 306 S.C. 252, 411 S.E.2d 223 (1991); State v. Livingston, 282 S.C. 1, 317 S.E.2d 129 (1984); State v. Johnson, 271 S.C. 485, 248 S.E.2d 313 (1978). The ten year limit was adopted to help guide trial courts in making uniform determinations in this area.

Subsection (c) regulates the effect of a pardon, annulment, certificate of rehabilitation or other equivalent procedures on the admissibility of a conviction for impeachment purposes. As to the effect of pardons issued by South Carolina, this subsection is arguably more restrictive than S.C. Code Ann. § 24-21-990(5) (Supp. 1993) which provides that a witness cannot be impeached by a conviction for which the witness received a pardon unless the crime indicates a lack of veracity.

The language of subsection (d) of the federal rule, which allows evidence of juvenile adjudications only in criminal cases and does not allow such evidence against the accused, was not used so that the South Carolina rule would conform with state law. Juvenile adjudications are admissible in this state to impeach any witness, including the accused, if the conduct would be criminal if it were committed by an adult. State v. Mallory, 270 S.C. 519, 242 S.E.2d 693 (1978). It should be noted that S.C. Code Ann. § 20-7-780 (Supp. 1993), which makes juvenile records confidential unless otherwise ordered by the family court, may limit access to records of juvenile adjudications.

No South Carolina authority existed as to the effect of the pendency of an appeal on the admissibility of evidence of the conviction. Subsection (e) of the federal rule was adopted verbatim.

RULE 610. RELIGIOUS BELIEFS OR OPINIONS

Evidence of the beliefs or opinions of a witness on matters of religion is not admissible for the purpose of showing that by reason of their nature the witness' credibility is impaired or enhanced.

Note:

No changes were made to the language of the federal rule. The South Carolina Supreme Court has held that a belief in God is not a prerequisite to allowing the witness to testify. State v. Green, 267 S.C. 599, 230 S.E.2d 618 (1976); State v. Hicks, 257 S.C. 279, 185 S.E.2d 746 (1971). However, in State v. Turner, 36 S.C. 534, 15 S.E. 602 (1892), the State was allowed to question the accused concerning comments ridiculing religion which he had allegedly made in order to impeach his credibility. This case is inconsistent with the rule.

RULE 611. MODE AND ORDER OF INTERROGATION AND PRESENTATION

(a) Control by Court. The court shall exercise reasonable control over the mode and order of interrogating witnesses and presenting evidence so as to (1) make the interrogation and presentation effective for the ascertainment of the truth, (2) avoid needless consumption of time, and (3) protect witnesses from harassment or undue embarrassment.

(b) Scope of Cross-Examination. A witness may be cross-examined on any matter relevant to any issue in the case, including credibility.

(c) Leading Questions. Leading questions should not be used on the direct examination of a witness except as may be necessary to develop the witness' testimony. Ordinarily leading questions should be permitted on cross-examination. When a party calls a hostile witness, an adverse party, or a witness identified with an adverse party, interrogation may be by leading questions.

(d) Re-examination and Recall. A witness may be re-examined as to the same matters to which he testified only in the discretion of the court, but without exception he may be re-examined as to any new matter brought out during cross-examination. After the examination of the witness has been concluded by all the parties to the action, that witness may be recalled only in the discretion of the court. This rule shall not limit the right of any party to recall a witness in rebuttal.

Note:

The language of subsection (a) of this rule is identical to that used in the federal rule. It is consistent with the general rule in this State that the conduct of the trial, including the examination of witnesses, is within the sound discretion of the trial judge. See McMillan v. Ridges, 229 S.C. 76, 91 S.E.2d 883 (1956); State v. Nathari, 303 S.C. 188, 399 S.E.2d 597 (Ct. App. 1990). It should be noted that Rule 614 controls the calling and interrogation of witnesses by the court.

Under South Carolina law, cross-examination is limited only by the requirement that the inquiry relate to matters pertinent to the issues involved or to impeachment of the witness. See State v. Ham, 259 S.C. 118, 191 S.E.2d 13 (1972); Hansson v. General Insulation and Acoustics, 234 S.C. 177, 107 S.E.2d 41 (1959). The scope of cross-examination is within the discretion of the trial judge. State v. Sherard, 303 S.C. 172, 399 S.E.2d 595 (1991). Subsection (b) rejects the more restrictive language of the federal rule which limits cross-examination to the subject matter of direct examination and matters affecting the credibility of the witness.

Subsection (c) is consistent with former law. See Rule 43(b)(1), SCRCP; Rule 43(b)(2), SCRCP. The use of leading questions when examining a child, State v. Hale, 284 S.C. 348, 326 S.E.2d 418 (Ct. App. 1985), cert. denied, 286 S.C. 127, 332 S.E.2d 533 (1985), is still permissible under the first sentence of subsection (c) which allows leading questions when "necessary to develop the witness' testimony."

There was no provision in the federal rule as to re-examination and recall of witnesses. The provision concerning re-examination and recall of witnesses was added to the rule to make it consistent with South Carolina law. See Levy v. Outdoor Resorts of South Carolina, Inc., 304 S.C. 427,

405 S.E.2d 387 (1991); State v. Stroman, 281 S.C. 508, 316 S.E.2d 395 (1984); Huff v. Latimer, 33 S.C. 255, 11 S.E. 758 (1890).

RULE 612. WRITING USED TO REFRESH MEMORY

If a witness uses a writing to refresh memory for the purpose of testifying, either -

(1) while testifying, or

(2) before testifying, if the court in its discretion determines it is necessary in the interests of justice,

an adverse party is entitled to have the writing produced at the hearing, to inspect it, to cross-examine the witness thereon, and to introduce in evidence those portions which relate to the testimony of the witness. If it is claimed that the writing contains matters not related to the subject matter of the testimony the court shall examine the writing in camera, excise any portions not so related, and order delivery of the remainder to the party entitled thereto. Any portion withheld over objections shall be preserved and made available to the appellate court in the event of an appeal. If a writing is not produced or delivered pursuant to order under this rule, the court shall make any order justice requires, except that in criminal cases when the prosecution elects not to comply, the order shall be one striking the testimony or, if the court in its discretion determines that the interests of justice so require, declaring a mistrial.

Note:
Except for the deletion of a reference to federal law, no changes were made to the federal rule. Requiring a party to provide a copy of a memorandum used by a witness to refresh recollection so that it may be used on cross-examination of the witness is consistent with prior law. State v. Hamilton, 276 S.C. 173, 276 S.E.2d 784 (1981); State v. Tyner, 273 S.C. 646, 258 S.E.2d 559 (1979). Rule 37(b)(2), SCRCP, and Rule 5(d)(2), SCRCrimP, are similar to the provision in this rule

concerning the trial judge's authority to decide the remedy for failure to produce a document for the adverse party.

RULE 613. PRIOR STATEMENTS OF WITNESSES

Subject to the provisions of S.C. Code Ann. §§ 19-1-80, 19-1-90 and 19-1-100:

(a) Examining Witness Concerning Prior Statement. In examining a witness concerning a prior statement made by the witness, whether written or not, the statement need not be shown nor its contents disclosed to the witness at that time, but on request the same shall be shown or disclosed to opposing counsel.

(b) Extrinsic Evidence of Prior Inconsistent Statement of Witness. Extrinsic evidence of a prior inconsistent statement by a witness is not admissible unless the witness is advised of the substance of the statement, the time and place it was allegedly made, and the person to whom it was made, and is given the opportunity to explain or deny the statement. If a witness does not admit that he has made the prior inconsistent statement, extrinsic evidence of such statement is admissible. However, if a witness admits making the prior statement, extrinsic evidence that the prior statement was made is inadmissible. This provision does not apply to admissions of a party-opponent as defined in Rule 801(d)(2).

Note:

The language at the beginning of this rule was added to provide that the rule is subject to the provisions of S.C. Code Ann. §§ 19-1-80 to -100 (1985) regarding written statements made to public employees.

Subsection (a) is identical to the federal rule. This provision was included in the federal rule to abolish the holding in The Queen's Case, 2 Br. & B. 284, 129 Eng. Rep. 976 (1820), that a witness must be shown a prior statement before being examined about the statement. Although no South Carolina case has been found adopting the holding in The Queen's

Case, the language of the federal rule eliminating the requirement of showing the witness the prior statement has been included in the South Carolina rule.

Subsection (b) of the federal rule was amended to provide that a proper foundation must be laid before admitting a prior inconsistent statement. A witness must be permitted to admit, deny, or explain a prior inconsistent statement. McMillan v. Ridges, 229 S.C. 76, 91 S.E.2d 883 (1956). Extrinsic evidence of the statement is not admissible unless the witness is advised of the substance of the statement, the time and place it was allegedly made, and the person to whom it was made. State v. Galloway, 263 S.C. 585, 211 S.E.2d 885 (1975). In addition, language was added to subsection (b) to set forth the rule that if the witness admits making the prior statement, the witness has been impeached and no further extrinsic evidence of the statement, including the statement itself, is admissible. State v. Lynn, 277 S.C. 222, 284 S.E.2d 786 (1981); McMillan v. Ridges, supra.

RULE 614. CALLING AND INTERROGATION OF WITNESSES BY COURT

(a) Calling by Court. In extraordinary circumstances, the court may, on its own motion or at the suggestion of a party, call witnesses, and all parties are entitled to cross-examine witnesses thus called. Before calling a court's witness, the court shall afford the parties a hearing on the matter outside the presence of the jury.

(b) Interrogation by Court. When required by the interests of justice only, the court may interrogate witnesses.

Note:
Subsection (a) is the federal rule modified in two respects. First, the phrase "[i]n extraordinary circumstances" was added to emphasize that under our adversarial system the decision whether to call a witness should generally be made by the parties, and the power of the court to call a witness ought to be sparingly used. The formulation of this rule differs from the rule established in State v. Anderson, 304 S.C. 551, 406

S.E.2d 152 (1991), although the circumstances in that case would be extraordinary circumstances justifying a court in calling a witness under this rule. Second, the federal rule was modified to require the court to afford the parties a hearing outside the presence of the jury before a witness is called by the court. This modification is consistent with prior case law. Id.; Riddle v. State, 314 S.C. 1, 443 S.E.2d 557 (1994). Allowing all parties to cross-examine a court's witness is also consistent with the prior case law. Riddle v. State, supra; State v. Anderson, supra.

Subsection (b) is the federal rule modified by adding the phrase "[w]hen required by the interests of justice only." This language was added to emphasize that this power, like the power to call a court's witness, should be used sparingly. If the court does interrogate a witness, the court must be careful not to intimate any opinion as to the force and effect of the testimony by its questions. Fowler v. Laney Tank Lines, Inc., 263 S.C. 422, 211 S.E.2d 231 (1975).

The federal rule contains a subsection (c) which may obviate the need for a timely objection to the calling of a court's witness or the interrogation of a witness by the court in certain circumstances. This provision is inconsistent with the law of South Carolina and was deleted. See State v. Torrence, 305 S.C. 45, 406 S.E.2d 315 (1991).

RULE 615. EXCLUSION OF WITNESSES

At the request of a party the court may order witnesses excluded so that they cannot hear the testimony of other witnesses, and it may make the order of its own motion. This rule does not authorize exclusion of (1) a party who is a natural person, or (2) an officer or employee of a party which is not a natural person designated as its representative by its attorney, or (3) a person whose presence is shown by a party to be essential to the presentation of the party's cause.

Note:
The federal rule requires sequestration of witnesses upon the request of a party. The South Carolina rule adheres to prior state practice which

leaves the sequestration decision in the sound discretion of the trial judge. See State v. Jackson, 265 S.C. 278, 217 S.E.2d 794 (1975); State v. Miokovich, 257 S.C. 225, 185 S.E.2d 360 (1971). Otherwise, the South Carolina rule is consistent with the federal rule.

Article VII. Opinions and Expert Testimony

RULE 701. OPINION TESTIMONY BY LAY WITNESSES

If the witness is not testifying as an expert, the witness' testimony in the form of opinions or inferences is limited to those opinions or inferences which (a) are rationally based on the perception of the witness, (b) are helpful to a clear understanding of the witness' testimony or the determination of a fact in issue, and (c) do not require special knowledge, skill, experience or training.

Note:

Except for the addition of subsection (c) and minor grammatical changes, this rule is identical to the federal rule. The language of subsection (c) is based on language contained in the rules of evidence of Florida and Tennessee, and is intended to emphasize the fact that lay persons may not give expert opinions.

Subsection (a) appears to be consistent with prior law. Cf. State v. Bottoms, 260 S.C. 187, 195 S.E.2d 116 (1973) (opinion must be based upon the personal observations of the witness and not merely upon the statements of another witness).

As to subsection (b), the prior case law has held that opinion evidence is admissible as long as it is not superfluous. State v. McClinton, 265 S.C. 171, 217 S.E.2d 584 (1974). This is roughly equivalent to saying that opinion evidence must be helpful.

As to subsection (c), the Court of Appeals has stated that expert testimony is essential where the topic is not a matter within the common knowledge and experience of most lay persons. Spartanburg Regional Med. Center v. Bulsa, 308 S.C. 322, 417 S.E.2d 648 (Ct. App. 1992); Armstrong v. Union Carbide, 308 S.C. 235, 417 S.E.2d 597 (Ct. App. 1992). Subsection (c) merely states this proposition in the reverse.

RULE 702. TESTIMONY BY EXPERTS

If scientific, technical, or other specialized knowledge will assist the trier of fact to understand the evidence or to determine a fact in issue, a witness qualified as an expert by knowledge, skill, experience, training, or education, may testify thereto in the form of an opinion or otherwise.

Note:

The rule is identical to the federal rule, and to former Rule 43(m)(1), SCRCP, and former Rule 24(a), SCRCrimP.

RULE 703. BASES OF OPINION TESTIMONY BY EXPERTS

The facts or data in the particular case upon which an expert bases an opinion or inference may be those perceived by or made known to the expert at or before the hearing. If of a type reasonably relied upon by experts in the particular field in forming opinions or inferences upon the subject, the facts or data need not be admissible in evidence.

Note:

The rule is identical to the federal rule and former Rule 43(m)(2), SCRCP, and former Rule 24(b), SCRCrimP. This rule makes it clear that an expert may rely on facts or data in giving an opinion which are not admitted into evidence.

RULE 704. OPINION ON ULTIMATE ISSUE

Testimony in the form of an opinion or inference otherwise admissible is not objectionable because it embraces an ultimate issue to be decided by the trier of fact.

Note:

This rule is identical to former Rule 43(m)(3), SCRCP, and former Rule 24(c), SCRCrimP. It is identical to the federal rule as it existed prior the

1984 amendment which added subsection (b) to the rule to prohibit expert testimony on the ultimate issue of whether a criminal defendant is insane.

RULE 705. DISCLOSURE OF FACTS OR DATA UNDERLYING EXPERT OPINION

The expert may testify in terms of opinion or inference and give reasons therefor without first testifying to the underlying facts or data, unless the court requires otherwise. The expert may in any event be required to disclose the underlying facts or data on cross-examination.

Note:

The rule is identical to the federal rule. It differs from former Rule 43(m)(4), SCRCP, and former Rule 24(d), SCRCrimP, which contained the phrase "without prior disclosure of" in place of the phrase "without first testifying to."

Article VIII. Hearsay

RULE 801. DEFINITIONS

The following definitions apply under this article:

(a) Statement. A "statement" is (1) an oral or written assertion or (2) nonverbal conduct of a person, if it is intended by the person as an assertion.

(b) Declarant. A "declarant" is a person who makes a statement.

(c) Hearsay. "Hearsay" is a statement, other than one made by the declarant while testifying at the trial or hearing, offered in evidence to prove the truth of the matter asserted.

(d) Statements Which Are Not Hearsay. A statement is not hearsay if -

(1) Prior Statement by Witness. The declarant testifies at the trial or hearing and is subject to cross-examination concerning the statement, and the statement is (A) inconsistent with the declarant's testimony, or (B) consistent with the declarant's testimony and is offered to rebut an express or implied charge against the declarant of recent fabrication or improper influence or motive; provided, however, the statement must have been made before the alleged fabrication, or before the alleged improper influence or motive arose, or (C) one of identification of a person made after perceiving the person, or (D) consistent with the declarant's testimony in a criminal sexual conduct case or attempted criminal sexual conduct case where the declarant is the alleged victim and the statement is limited to the time and place of the incident; or

(2) Admission by Party-Opponent. The statement is offered against a party and is (A) the party's own statement in either an individual or a representative capacity, or (B) a statement of which the party has manifested an adoption or belief in its truth, or (C) a statement by a person authorized by the party to make a statement concerning the subject, or (D) a statement by the party's agent or servant concerning a matter within the scope of the agency or employment, made during the existence of the relationship, or (E) a statement by a coconspirator of a party during the course and in furtherance of the conspiracy.

Note:

With the exception of subsection (d)(1), this rule is identical to the federal rule.

While case law has not defined the words "statement" and "declarant," the definitions in subsections (a) and (b) are consistent with how those words are used in numerous cases discussing the hearsay rule. Prior law recognized that wordless conduct intended as a communication may be hearsay. State v. Williams, 285 S.C. 544, 331 S.E.2d 354 (Ct. App. 1985).

Subsection (c) is consistent with South Carolina law. Player v. Thompson, 259 S.C. 600, 193 S.E.2d 531 (1972).

Subsection (d)(1) changes the law in South Carolina. Previously, where the declarant testified at trial and was subject to cross-examination, the general rule was that prior statements made by the declarant/witness were admissible regardless of the hearsay nature of the statements. See State v. Garner, 304 S.C. 220, 403 S.E.2d 631 (1991); State v. Caldwell, 283 S.C. 350, 322 S.E.2d 662 (1984); State v. Plyler, 275 S.C. 291, 270 S.E.2d 126 (1980); but see State v. Munn, 292 S.C. 497, 357 S.E.2d 461 (1987) (all out-of-court statements made by alleged victim not necessarily admissible simply because victim testifies at trial). Subsection (d)(1), however, treats prior statements of a witness as not being hearsay in only four instances. Subsection (A) omits the requirement of the federal rule that the declarant's prior inconsistent statement be given under oath. This modification renders the rule consistent with South Carolina law. See State v. Copeland, 278 S.C. 572, 300 S.E.2d 63 (1982), cert. denied, 460 U.S. 1103, 103 S.Ct. 1802, 76 L.Ed.2d 367 (1983). It should be noted that the foundation requirements of Rule 613(b) must be met before extrinsic evidence of a prior inconsistent statement is admissible. Subsection (B) is the federal rule modified by adding the phrase "provided, however, the statement must have been made before the alleged fabrication, or before the alleged improper influence or motive arose." This modification, which is taken from the United States Supreme Court's interpretation of Rule 801(d)(1)(B) of the Federal Rules of Evidence in Tome v. United States, 513 U.S. 150, 130 L.Ed.2d 574, 115 S.Ct. 696 (1995), is somewhat similar to the limitation previously contained in the case law that a prior consistent statement is admissible only where it was made prior to the declarant's relation to the cause. Jolly v. State, 314 S.C. 17, 443 S.E.2d 566 (1994); Burns v. Clayton, 237 S.C. 316, 117 S.E.2d 300 (1960). Subsection (C) is identical to the federal rule and consistent with South Carolina law that evidence regarding pre-trial identifications, which are not the product of unconstitutional procedures, are admissible. State v. Stewart, 275 S.C. 447, 272 S.E.2d 628 (1980); State v. Gambrell, 274 S.C. 587, 266 S.E.2d 78 (1980). Subsection (D), which is not contained in the federal rule, was added to make admissible in criminal sexual conduct cases evidence that the victim complained of the sexual assault, limited to the time and place of the assault. Subsection (D) is consistent with South Carolina law. Jolly v. State, 314 S.C. 17, 443 S.E.2d 566 (1994).

Subsection (d)(2)(A) is consistent with South Carolina law. Bunch v. Cobb, 273 S.C. 445, 257 S.E.2d 225 (1979) (admission against interest of a party opponent is admissible); State v. Good, 308 S.C. 313, 417 S.E.2d 643 (Ct. App. 1992) (an out of court admission of a criminal defendant is admissible). Subsection (B) is consistent with South Carolina law. State v. Sharpe, 239 S.C. 258, 122 S.E.2d 622 (1962) (testimony that defendant was silent in response to an accusation by a third party admissible), rev'd on other grounds, State v. Torrence, 305 S.C. 45, 406 S.E.2d 315 (1991); Coleman & Lipscomb v. Frazier, 38 S.C.L. (4 Rich.) 146 (1850) (where party received a statement and acted on it as true, statement admissible). Subsection (C) is consistent with South Carolina law. Harper v. American Ry. Express Co., 139 S.C. 545, 138 S.E. 354 (1927) (statements by a person authorized to speak are admissible). Subsection (D) is consistent with South Carolina law that statements made by an agent in the scope of his authority were admissible. Hunter v. Hyder, 236 S.C. 378, 114 S.E.2d 493 (1960). Subsection (E) is consistent with South Carolina law. State v. Sullivan, 277 S.C. 35, 282 S.E.2d 838 (1981); Yeager v. Murphy, 291 S.C. 485, 354 S.E.2d 393 (Ct. App. 1987) (statements made by co-conspirators in furtherance of the conspiracy are admissible).

RULE 802. HEARSAY RULE

Hearsay is not admissible except as provided by these rules or by other rules prescribed by the Supreme Court of this State or by statute.

Note:

The rule replaces the words "by the Supreme Court pursuant to statutory authority or by Act of Congress" found in the federal rule with "by the Supreme Court of this State or by statute." It is consistent with the general rule that hearsay is not admissible unless it fits within an exception to the hearsay rule. Jolly v. State, 314 S.C. 17, 443 S.E.2d 566 (1994); Lee v. Gulf Ins. Co., 248 S.C. 296, 149 S.E.2d 639 (1966).

RULE 803. HEARSAY EXCEPTIONS; AVAILABILITY OF ECLARANT IMMATERIAL

The following are not excluded by the hearsay rule, even though the declarant is available as a witness:

(1) Present Sense Impression. A statement describing or explaining an event or condition made while the declarant was perceiving the event or condition, or immediately thereafter.

(2) Excited Utterance. A statement relating to a startling event or condition made while the declarant was under the stress of excitement caused by the event or condition.

(3) Then Existing Mental, Emotional, or Physical Condition. A statement of the declarant's then existing state of mind, emotion, sensation, or physical condition (such as intent, plan, motive, design, mental feeling, pain, and bodily health), but not including a statement of memory or belief to prove the fact remembered or believed unless it relates to the execution, revocation, identification, or terms of declarant's will.

(4) Statements for Purposes of Medical Diagnosis or Treatment. Statements made for purposes of medical diagnosis or treatment and describing medical history, or past or present symptoms, pain, or sensations, or the inception or general character of the cause or external source thereof insofar as reasonably pertinent to diagnosis or treatment; provided, however, that the admissibility of statements made after commencement of the litigation is left to the court's discretion.

(5) Recorded Recollection. A memorandum or record concerning a matter about which a witness once had knowledge but now has insufficient recollection to enable the witness to testify fully and accurately, shown to have been made or adopted by the witness when the matter was fresh in the witness' memory and to reflect that knowledge correctly. If admitted, the memorandum or record may be read into evidence but may not itself be received as an exhibit unless offered by an adverse party.

(6) Records of Regularly Conducted Activity. A memorandum, report, record, or data compilation, in any form, of acts, events, conditions, or diagnoses, made at or near the time by, or from information transmitted by, a person with knowledge, if kept in the course of a regularly conducted business activity, and if it was the regular practice of that business activity to make the memorandum, report, record, or data compilation, all as shown by the testimony of the custodian or other qualified witness, unless the source of information or the method or circumstances of preparation indicate lack of trustworthiness; provided, however, that subjective opinions and judgments found in business records are not admissible. The term "business" as used in this subsection includes business, institution, association, profession, occupation, and calling of every kind, whether or not conducted for profit.

(7) Absence of Entry in Records Kept in Accordance With the Provisions of Subsection (6). Evidence that a matter is not included in the memoranda, reports, records, or data compilations, in any form, kept in accordance with the provisions of subsection (6), to prove the nonoccurrence or nonexistence of the matter, if the matter was of a kind of which a memorandum, report, record, or data compilation was regularly made and preserved, unless the sources of information or other circumstances indicate lack of trustworthiness.

(8) Public Records and Reports. Records, reports, statements, or data compilations, in any form, of public offices or agencies, setting forth (A) the activities of the office or agency, or (B) matters observed pursuant to duty imposed by law as to which matters there was a duty to report, excluding, however, in criminal cases matters observed by police officers and other law enforcement personnel; <u>provided</u>, <u>however</u>, that investigative notes involving opinions, judgments, or conclusions are not admissible. Accident reports required by S.C. Code Ann. §§ 56-5-1260 to -1280 (1991) are not admissible as evidence of negligence or due care in an action at law for damages.

(9) Records of Vital Statistics. Records or data compilations, in any form, of births, fetal deaths, deaths, or marriages, if the report thereof was made to a public office pursuant to requirements of law.

(10) Absence of Public Record or Entry. To prove the absence of a record, report, statement, or data compilation, in any form, or the nonoccurrence or nonexistence of a matter of which a record, report, statement or data compilation, in any form, was regularly made and preserved by a public office or agency, evidence in the form of a certification in accordance with Rule 902, or testimony, that diligent search failed to disclose the record, report, statement, or data compilation, or entry.

(11) Records of Religious Organizations. Statements of births, marriages, divorces, deaths, legitimacy, ancestry, relationship by blood or marriage, or other similar facts of personal or family history, contained in a regularly kept record of a religious organization.

(12) Marriage, Baptismal, and Similar Certificates. Statements of fact contained in a certificate that the maker performed a marriage or other ceremony or administered a sacrament, made by a clergyman, public official, or other person authorized by the rules or practices of a religious organization or by law to perform the act certified, and purporting to have been issued at the time of the act or within a reasonable time thereafter.

(13) Family Records. Statements of fact concerning personal or family history contained in family Bibles, genealogies, charts, engravings on rings, inscriptions on family portraits, engravings on urns, crypts, or tombstones, or the like.

(14) Records of Documents Affecting an Interest in Property. The record of a document purporting to establish or affect an interest in property, as proof of the content of the original recorded document and its execution and delivery by each person by whom it purports to have been executed, if the record is a record of a public office and an applicable statute authorizes the recording of documents of that kind in that office.

(15) Statements in Documents Affecting an Interest in Property. A statement contained in a document purporting to establish or affect an interest in property if the matter stated was relevant to the purpose of the document, unless dealings with the property since the document was made have been inconsistent with the truth of the statement or the purport of the document.

(16) Statements in Ancient Documents. Statements in a document in existence twenty years or more the authenticity of which is established.

(17) Market Reports, Commercial Publications. Market quotations, tabulations, lists, directories, or other published compilations, generally used and relied upon by the public or by persons in particular occupations.

(18) Learned Treatises. To the extent called to the attention of an expert witness upon cross-examination or relied upon by the expert witness in direct examination, statements contained in published treatises, periodicals, or pamphlets on a subject of history, medicine, or other science or art, established as a reliable authority by the testimony or admission of the witness or by other expert testimony or by judicial notice. If admitted, the statements may be read into evidence but may not be received as exhibits. This rule is in addition to any statutory provisions on this subject.

(19) Reputation Concerning Personal or Family History. Reputation among members of a person's family by blood, adoption, or marriage, or among a person's associates, or in the community, concerning a person's birth, adoption, marriage, divorce, death, legitimacy, relationship by blood, adoption, or marriage, ancestry, or other similar fact of personal or family history.

(20) Reputation Concerning Boundaries or General History. Reputation in a community, arising before the controversy, as to boundaries of or customs affecting lands in the community, and reputation as to events of general history important to the community or State or nation in which located.

(21) Reputation as to Character. Reputation of a person's character among associates or in the community.

(22) Judgment of Previous Conviction. Evidence of a final judgment (to include final judgments in juvenile delinquency matters), entered after a trial or upon a plea of guilty (but not upon a plea of nolo contendere), adjudging a person guilty of a crime punishable by death or imprisonment in excess of one year, to prove any fact essential to sustain the judgment, but not including, when offered by the Government in a criminal prosecution for purposes other than impeachment, judgments against persons other than the accused. The pendency of an appeal may be shown but does not affect admissibility.

(23) Judgment as to Personal, Family or General History, or Boundaries. Judgments as proof of matters of personal, family or general history, or boundaries, essential to the judgment, if the same would be provable by evidence of reputation.

Note:

Except for modifications to subsections (4), (6), (8), (18), and (22), and the deletion of subsection (24) which contained a "catchall" or residual hearsay exception, this rule is identical to the federal rule.

Subsections (1) and (2): These subsections constitute a change in South Carolina law. Previously, a statement had to meet the conditions of both subsections (1) and (2) before it would be admissible under the res gestae exception to the hearsay rule. State v. Harrison, 298 S.C. 333, 380 S.E.2d 818 (1989).

Subsection (3): This subsection is consistent with prior state practice. Winburn v. Minnesota Mut. Life Ins. Co., 261 S.C. 568, 201 S.E.2d 372 (1973); Sligh v. Newberry Elec. Coop.,Inc., 216 S.C. 401, 58 S.E.2d 675 (1950); Ervin v. Myrtle Grove Plantation, 206 S.C. 41, 32 S.E.2d 877 (1945); Lazar v. Great Atl.& Pac. Tea Co., 197 S.C. 74, 14 S.E.2d 560 (1941); Spires v. Spires, 111 S.C. 373, 97 S.E. 847 (1919).

Subsection (4): The first part of this subsection is identical to the federal rule and is consistent with state practice. State v. Camele, 293 S.C. 302, 360 S.E.2d 307 (1987) (physician's testimony should include only those statements related to him by the patient upon which the physician relied in reaching medical conclusions); Gentry v. Watkins-Carolina Trucking Co., 249 S.C. 316, 154 S.E.2d 112 (1967) (statements of present condition and past symptoms made to a physician consulted as a potential witness are admissible, not as substantive evidence, but, in the absence of fraud or bad faith, as information upon which the physician relied in reaching a professional opinion). The final phrase was added to the subsection to provide that the admissibility of statements made after commencement of the litigation is within the trial judge's discretion. Gentry v. Watkins-Carolina Trucking Co., supra.

Subsection (5): This subsection is similar to previous state law which allowed a witness to testify from a writing when it was the original document prepared by the witness contemporaneously with the event for the purpose of preserving the memory of it. Gwathmey v. Foor Hotel Co., 121 S.C. 237, 113 S.E. 688 (1922); The Bank of Charleston Nat'l Banking Ass'n v. Zorn, 14 S.C. 444 (1881). The provision of this rule limiting the introduction of the writing to when it is offered by an adverse party is a change in South Carolina law.

Subsection (6): This subsection differs from the federal rule in that the word "opinions" in the first sentence is deleted and the phrase, "provided, however, that subjective opinions and judgments found in business records are not admissible" is added to the federal rule to make it consistent with state law. Kershaw County Dep't of Social Serv. v. McCaskill, 276 S.C. 360, 278 S.E.2d 771 (1981); see also State v. Rich, 293 S.C. 172, 359 S.E.2d 281 (1987) (admission of properly authenticated fingerprints); Uniform Business Records as Evidence Act, S.C. Code Ann. § 19-5-510 (1985).

Subsection (7): While the case law has recognized the admissibility of negative evidence to prove the non-existence of records of regularly conducted activity, the courts have not recognized this as a separate hearsay exception. E.g., Peoples Nat'l Bank v. Manos Bros., Inc., 226 S.C. 257, 84 S.E.2d 857 (1955); see also Flowers v. South Carolina Dep't of Highways and Pub. Transp., 309 S.C. 76, 419 S.E.2d 832 (Ct. App. 1992) (citing federal rule).

Subsection (8): This subsection differs from the federal rule in that it does not include item (C). The subsection also contains two limitations not included in the federal rule. First, investigative notes involving opinions, judgments, or conclusions are not admissible. Further, accident reports required by statute are not admissible as evidence of negligence or due care in actions for damages. As modified, this subsection is consistent with prior state practice. State v. Pearson, 223 S.C. 377, 76 S.E.2d 151 (1953); S.C. Code Ann. § 56-5-1290 (1991); see also State v. Rich, 293

S.C. 172, 359 S.E.2d 281 (1987) (admission of properly authenticated fingerprints).

Subsection (9): This subsection constitutes a change in South Carolina law. Prior case law limited admissions of such reports to matters within the knowledge of the person making the report. Williams v. Metropolitan Life Ins. Co., 116 S.C. 277, 108 S.E. 110 (1921).

Subsection (10): While the case law has recognized the admissibility of negative evidence to prove the non-existence of public records, the courts have not recognized this as a separate hearsay exception. See Peoples Nat'l Bank v. Manos Bros., Inc., 226 S.C. 257, 84 S.E.2d 857 (1955) (introduction of evidence of the non-existence of public record entries); Flowers v. South Carolina Dep't of Highways and Pub. Transp., 309 S.C. 76, 419 S.E.2d 832 (Ct.App.1992) (citing federal rule). See also Rule 44(b), SCRCP.

Subsection (11): There does not appear to be any South Carolina law concerning this exception to the hearsay rule.

Subsection (12): No prior South Carolina authority has been found which states the hearsay exception expressed in this subsection.

Subsection (13): This exception is apparently consistent with prior case law in this State. See Dobson v. Cothran, 34 S.C. 518, 13 S.E. 679 (1891) (entry in family Bible of the birth date of a person is admissible as evidence of the person's age only where better evidence cannot be obtained).

Subsection (14): This subsection is consistent with statutory and case law in this State. Wilson v. Moseley, 113 S.C. 278, 102 S.E. 330 (1920) (a record book from a clerk's office, wherein a deed was authorized to be recorded and was recorded, is admissible to prove the existence and contents of the deed if sufficient evidence is presented to prove that the original deed is not available); S.C. Code Ann. § 19-5-10 (1985) (admissibility of certified copies or certified photostatic copies of documents).

Subsection (15): This provision is apparently consistent with prior case law in this State. See Smith v. Williams, 141 S.C. 265, 139 S.E. 625 (1927) (husband's statements in a deed and accompanying memorandum purporting to convey an interest in property admissible to show whether family agreement had been made following husband's death entitling widow to retain use and possession of the property).

Subsection (16): The ancient document exception to the hearsay rule in subsection (16) is consistent with prior case law in this State. However, prior case law qualified a document as "ancient" if the document was thirty years old or older. Atlantic Coast Line R.R. Co. v. Searson, 137 S.C. 468, 135 S.E. 567 (1926) (map more than thirty years old could be introduced as ancient document); Johnson v. Pritchard, 302 S.C. 437, 395 S.E.2d 191 (Ct. App. 1990) (duly authenticated ancient documents of thirty years or more constitute an exception to the hearsay rule). Subsection (16) qualifies a document as "ancient" if it is twenty years old or older.

Subsection (17): This provision is consistent with prior case law in this State. Peoples Nat'l Bank v. Manos Bros., Inc., 226 S.C. 257, 84 S.E.2d 857 (1954) (on the issue of domicile, a city directory is admissible); Kirkpatrick v. Hardeman, 123 S.C. 21, 115 S.E. 905 (1923) (accredited current price lists and market reports, including those published in trade journals or newspapers, which are accepted as trustworthy, are admissible on the question of market value of stock).

Subsection (18): This exception is identical to the federal rule except for the addition of the last sentence. This rule changes and expands previous South Carolina law which held that medical books are not admissible into evidence to be read to the court and jury except in the situations set forth in S.C. Code Ann. § 19-5-410 (1985).See LaCount v. General Asbestos & Rubber Co., 184 S.C. 232, 192 S.E. 262 (1937); Baker v. Southern Cotton Oil Co., 161 S.C. 479, 159 S.E. 822 (1931); Edwards v. Union Buffalo Mills Co., 162 S.C. 17, 159 S.E. 818 (1931). This rule is consistent with the case of Baker v. Port City Steel Erectors, Inc., 261 S.C. 469, 200

S.E.2d 681 (1973), which states that a scientific textbook can be used for the purpose of impeaching an expert witness.

Subsection (19): This exception is consistent with prior state law. Hazelwood v. Mayes, 111 S.C. 23, 96 S.E. 672 (1918); Horry v. Glover, 11 S.C.Eq. (2 Hill Eq.) 515 (1837).

Subsection (20): This exception is consistent with prior state law. Culbertson v. Culbertson, 273 S.C. 103, 254 S.E.2d 558 (1979) (boundary); County of Darlington v. Perkins, 269 S.C. 572, 239 S.E.2d 69 (1977) (general history).

Subsection (21): There is no South Carolina law dealing with this exception. This section is included in the rules to insure that reputation evidence is not excluded on the basis of hearsay. See Weinstein's Evidence ¶ 803(21)[01] (1994). Rules 404, 405, and 608 deal with when reputation evidence may be admissible.

Subsection (22): This subsection is identical to the federal rule except for the addition of the phrase "to include final judgments in juvenile delinquency matters." This addition makes it clear that a final judgment in a juvenile delinquency matter is to be treated in the same manner as an adult conviction under this subsection; to determine if the crime is punishable by death or imprisonment in excess of one year, the maximum punishment an adult would receive for the offense is controlling. Traditionally, evidence of a judgment in a criminal case was not admissible in a civil case as evidence of the facts upon which the conviction was based. Fontville v. Atlanta & Charlotte Air Line Ry. Co., 93 S.C. 287, 75 S.E. 172 (1910). This traditional rule has, however, been eroded in several cases. South Carolina State Board of Dental Examiners v. Breeland, 208 S.C. 469, 38 S.E.2d 644 (1946) (at least where the police power of the state is involved in a civil case, a criminal conviction based on a jury verdict is admissible); Globe & Rutgers Fire Ins. Co. v. Foil, 189 S.C. 91, 200 S.E. 97 (1938) (evidence of a conviction based on a guilty plea is admissible in a civil case as an admission against the criminal defendant). The adoption of this rule now allows criminal judgments based on a plea of guilty or a trial for an offense which carries a maximum punishment of death or imprisonment for more than one year to be admissible in almost all civil actions to prove the facts essential to the criminal judgment. Not allowing a criminal judgment based on a plea of nolo contendere to be used to prove the facts on which the judgment is based is consistent with the prior case law. <u>Kibler v. State</u>, 267 S.C. 250, 227 S.E.2d 199 (1976) (plea of nolo cannot be used as an admission in a civil case); <u>see also</u> <u>In re Anderson</u>, 255 S.C. 56, 177 S.E.2d 130 (1970) (attorney disciplinary proceeding). It should be noted that S.C. Code Ann. § 56-5-6160 (1991) limits the admissibility of evidence of a conviction for a traffic offense. Further, S.C. Code Ann. § 20-7-780 (Supp. 1993), which makes juvenile records confidential unless otherwise ordered by the family court, may limit access to final judgments in juvenile delinquency matters.

Subsection (23): This exception is consistent with prior state law. <u>Bradley v. Calhoun</u>, 116 S.C. 7, 106 S.E. 843 (1921).

RULE 804. HEARSAY EXCEPTIONS; DECLARANT UNAVAILABLE

(a) Definition of Unavailability. "Unavailability as a witness" includes situations in which the declarant -

(1) is exempted by ruling of the court on the ground of privilege from testifying concerning the subject matter of the declarant's statement; or

(2) persists in refusing to testify concerning the subject matter of the declarant's statement despite an order of the court to do so; or

(3) testifies to a lack of memory of the subject matter of the declarant's statement; or

(4) is unable to be present or to testify at the hearing because of death or then existing physical or mental illness or infirmity; or

(5) is absent from the hearing and the proponent of a statement has been unable to procure the declarant's attendance (or in the case of a hearsay exception under subdivision (b)(2), (3), or (4), the declarant's attendance or testimony) by process or other reasonable means.

A declarant is not unavailable as a witness if exemption, refusal, claim of lack of memory, inability, or absence is due to the procurement or wrongdoing of the proponent of a statement for the purpose of preventing the witness from attending or testifying.

(b) Hearsay Exceptions. The following are not excluded by the hearsay rule if the declarant is unavailable as a witness:

(1) Former Testimony. Testimony given as a witness at another hearing of the same or a different proceeding, or in a deposition taken in compliance with law in the course of the same or another proceeding, if the party against whom the testimony is now offered, or, in a civil action or proceeding, a predecessor in interest, had an opportunity and similar motive to develop the testimony by direct, cross, or redirect examination.

(2) Statement Under Belief of Impending Death. In a prosecution for homicide or in a civil action or proceeding, a statement made by a declarant while believing that the declarant's death was imminent, concerning the cause or circumstances of what the declarant believed to be impending death.

(3) Statement Against Interest. A statement which was at the time of its making so far contrary to the declarant's pecuniary or proprietary interest, or so far tended to subject the declarant to civil or criminal liability, or to render invalid a claim by the declarant against another, that a reasonable person in the declarant's position would not have made the statement unless believing it to be true. A statement tending to expose the declarant to criminal liability and offered to exculpate the accused is not admissible unless corroborating circumstances clearly indicate the trustworthiness of the statement.

(4) Statement of Personal or Family History. (A) A statement concerning the declarant's own birth, adoption, marriage, divorce, legitimacy, relationship by blood, adoption, or marriage, ancestry, or other similar fact of personal or family history, even though declarant had no means of acquiring personal knowledge of the matter stated; or (B) a statement concerning the foregoing matters, and death also, of another person, if the declarant was related to the other by blood, adoption, or marriage or was so intimately associated with the other's family as to be likely to have accurate information concerning the matter declared.

Note:

Subsection (a) is identical to the federal rule and consistent with South Carolina law. Riddle v. State, 314 S.C. 1, 443 S.E.2d 557 (1994) (witness unavailable who refuses to testify even after being threatened with contempt); State v. Doctor, 306 S.C. 527, 413 S.E.2d 36 (1992) (witness who asserts a privilege is unavailable); State v. Steadman, 216 S.C. 579, 59 S.E.2d 168, cert. denied, 340 U.S. 850, 71 S.Ct. 78, 95 L.Ed. 623 (1950) (witness who is absent from the jurisdiction and cannot be found is unavailable); State v. Rogers, 101 S.C. 280, 85 S.E. 636 (1914) (witness who is dead, insane, beyond the seas, or kept away by the contrivance of the opposing party is unavailable).

Subsection (b) omits subsection (5), the "catch all" or residual hearsay exception found in the federal rule, but is otherwise identical to the federal rule. Subsection (1) is consistent with South Carolina law. State v. Steadman, 216 S.C. 579, 59 S.E.2d 168, cert. denied, 340 U.S. 850, 71 S.Ct. 78, 95 L.Ed. 623 (1950). It should be noted that S.C. Code Ann. § 19-11-50 (1985), which provides that the testimony of a criminal defendant may not be used in any subsequent criminal case against him except prosecution for perjury founded on that testimony, may place some limit on the admissibility of evidence under this subsection. Subsection (2) broadens the admissibility of dying declarations by making them admissible in civil cases. See Sligh v. Newberry Electric Co-op., 216 S.C. 401, 58 S.E.2d 675 (1950). The rigid requirement that the declarant must actually have died, State v. Dawson, 203 S.C. 167, 26 S.E.2d 506 (1943), is relaxed under the Rule which only requires the death of the declarant in a homicide prosecution. Subsection (3) is consistent with South Carolina law. State v. Doctor, 306 S.C. 527, 413 S.E.2d 36 (1992).

Subsection (4) is consistent with South Carolina law. McLain v. Woodside, 95 S.C. 152, 79 S.E. 1 (1913).

RULE 805. HEARSAY WITHIN HEARSAY

Hearsay included within hearsay is not excluded under the hearsay rule if each part of the combined statements conforms with an exception to the hearsay rule provided in these rules.

Note:

The rule is identical to the federal rule and is consistent with prior South Carolina case law. Bain v. Self Memorial Hosp., 281 S.C. 138, 314 S.E.2d 603 (Ct. App. 1984).

RULE 806. ATTACKING AND SUPPORTING CREDIBILITY OF DECLARANT

When a hearsay statement, or a statement defined in Rule 801(d)(2)(C), (D), or (E) has been admitted in evidence, the credibility of the declarant may be attacked, and if attacked may be supported, by any evidence which would be admissible for those purposes if declarant had testified as a witness. Evidence of a statement or conduct by the declarant at any time, inconsistent with the declarant's hearsay statement, is not subject to any requirement that the declarant may have been afforded an opportunity to deny or explain. If the party against whom a hearsay statement has been admitted calls the declarant as a witness, the party is entitled to examine the declarant on the statement as if under cross-examination.

Note:

The rule is identical to the federal rule. However, it is a departure from prior South Carolina case law. There are cases which have addressed a similar matter by holding that a declarant who made a dying declaration could not be impeached with an inconsistent statement that did not independently fall within a hearsay exception. State v. Brown, 108 S.C. 490, 95 S.E. 61 (1918); State v. Taylor, 56 S.C. 360, 34 S.E. 939 (1900).

Article IX. Authentication and Identification

RULE 901. REQUIREMENT OF AUTHENTICATION OR IDENTIFICATION

(a) General Provision. The requirement of authentication or identification as a condition precedent to admissibility is satisfied by evidence sufficient to support a finding that the matter in question is what its proponent claims.

(b) Illustrations. By way of illustration only, and not by way of limitation, the following are examples of authentication or identification conforming with the requirements of this rule:

(1) Testimony of Witness With Knowledge. Testimony that a matter is what it is claimed to be.

(2) Nonexpert Opinion on Handwriting. Non-expert opinion as to the genuineness of handwriting, based upon familiarity not acquired for purposes of the litigation.

(3) Comparison by Trier or Expert Witness. Comparison by the trier of fact or by expert witnesses with specimens which have been authenticated.

(4) Distinctive Characteristics and the Like. Appearance, contents, substance, internal patterns, or other distinctive characteristics, taken in conjunction with circumstances.

(5) Voice Identification. Identification of a voice, whether heard firsthand or through mechanical or electronic transmission or recording, by opinion based upon hearing the voice at any time under circumstances connecting it with the alleged speaker.

(6) Telephone Conversations. Telephone conversations, by evidence that a call was made to the number assigned at the time by the telephone company to a particular person or business, if (A) in the case of a person, circumstances, including self-identification, show the person answering to be the one called, or (B) in the case of a business, the call was made to a place of business and the conversation related to business reasonably transacted over the telephone.

(7) Public Records or Reports. Evidence that a writing authorized by law to be recorded or filed and in fact recorded or filed in a public office, or a purported public record, report, statement, or data compilation, in any form, is from the public office where items of this nature are kept.

(8) Ancient Documents or Data Compilation. Evidence that a document or data compilation, in any form, (A) is in such condition as to create no suspicion concerning its authenticity, (B) was in a place where it, if authentic, would likely be, and (C) has been in existence 20 years or more at the time it is offered.

(9) Process or System. Evidence describing a process or system used to produce a result and showing that the process or system produces an accurate result.

(10) Methods Provided by Statute or Rule. Any method of authentication or identification provided by statute or by other rules promulgated by the Supreme Court.

Note:
In considering the rules in Article IX, it is important to remember that these rules relate to how a party authenticates evidence to show it is what the party claims. Even when evidence is properly authenticated, it must still be admissible under the other rules of evidence. See State v. Jeffcoat, 279 S.C. 167, 303 S.E.2d 855 (1983).

With the exception of subsection (b)(10) which is discussed below, this rule is identical to the federal rule.

Subsection (a) is consistent with South Carolina law which requires authentication as a condition precedent to admissibility. See State v. Rich, 293 S.C. 172, 359 S.E.2d 281 (1987). As noted in the Advisory Committee's Notes to the Federal Rules, the requirement of showing authentication or identity falls in the category of relevancy dependent upon fulfillment of a condition of fact and is governed by the procedure set forth in Rule 104(b).

Subsection (b) contains illustrations of how evidence may be authenticated. These illustrations are consistent with the prior case law indicating that evidence in support of authentication can be direct or circumstantial. Winburn v. Minnesota Mutual Life Ins. Co., 261 S.C. 568, 201 S.E.2d 372 (1973); State v. Wilson, 246 S.C. 580, 145 S.E.2d 20 (1965).

Subsection (b)(1) is in accord with the prior law in this state. Williams v. Milling-Nelson Motors, Inc., 209 S.C. 407, 40 S.E.2d 633 (1946); Brazeale v. Piedmont Mfg. Co., 184 S.C. 471, 193 S.E. 99 (1937).

Subsection (b)(2) is generally consistent with state law State v. Jeffcoat, 279 S.C. 167, 303 S.E.2d 855 (1983) (signature on check identified by signatory's bookkeeper); Weaver v. Whilden, 33 S.C. 190, 11 S.E. 686 (1890) (no error in refusing to allow nonexpert witness who was unfamiliar with handwriting to testify as to genuineness of signature). There does not appear to be any South Carolina law that states that the familiarity cannot have been acquired for the purposes of litigation.

Subsection (b)(3) is in accord with the prior case law in South Carolina. Pee Dee Production Credit Ass'n v. Joye, 284 S.C. 371, 326 S.E.2d 650 (1984); Benedict, Hall & Co. v. Flanigan, 18 S.C. 506 (1883); Boman v. Plunkett, 13 S.C.L. (2 McCord) 518 (1823) (comparison by jury was permitted in aid of doubtful proof). South Carolina has also recognized that nonexperts can make such comparisons. State v. Ezekiel, 33 S.C. 115, 11 S.E. 635 (1890); Benedict, Hall & Co. v. Flanigan, 18 S.C. 506 (1883).

Subsection (b)(4) is consistent with prior law. Kershaw, City. Bd. of Educ. v. U.S. Gypsum, 302 S.C. 390, 396 S.E.2d 369 (1990); IKT Company Inc. v. Hardwick, 274 S.C. 413, 265 S.E.2d 510 (1980); State v. Hightower, 221 S.C. 91, 69 S.E.2d 363 (1952). A common form of authentication permissible under this subsection is the reply doctrine which provides that once a letter, telegram, or telephone call is shown to have been mailed, sent, or made, a letter, telegram or telephone call shown by its contents to be in reply is authenticated without more. Graham, Handbook of Federal Evidence, § 901.4 (2nd ed. 1986). This appears to be the law in South Carolina. Leesville Mfg. Co. v. Morgan Wood & Iron Works, 75 S.C. 342, 55 S.E. 768 (1906) (reply letter is presumed genuine).

Subsection (b)(5) is consistent with the law in South Carolina. State v. Stewart, 275 S.C. 447, 272 S.E.2d 628 (1980) (identification of defendant's voice as that of armed robber was admissible in criminal prosecution where circumstances demonstrate reliability of evidence); State v. Plyler, 275 S.C. 291, 270 S.E.2d 126 (1980) (sufficient testimony as to recognition of the voice warrants its admission); State v. Vice, 259 S.C. 30, 190 S.E.2d 510 (1972) (voice identification permissible; further, jury can compare recorded telephone call and defendant's voice, recorded prior to trial, for purposes of comparison); State v. Porter, 251 S.C. 393, 162 S.E.2d 843 (1968) (identification of party with whom witness talked need not be known at time of conversation, but is sufficient if knowledge enabling witness to identify other party is later obtained), cert. denied, 393 U.S. 1079, 89 S.Ct. 859, 21 L.Ed.2d 773 (1969); State v. Steadman, 216 S.C. 579, 59 S.E.2d 168 (1950); State v. Smith, 307 S.C. 376, 415 S.E.2d 409 (Ct.App.1992) (dispatcher allowed to identify voice of anonymous caller as that of defendant, even though no prior voice identification training).

Subsection (b)(6) is in accord with the prior law in this State. Fielding Home for Funerals v. Pub. Sav. Life Ins. Co., 271 S.C. 117, 245 S.E.2d 238 (1978) (business); State v. Steadman, 216 S.C. 579, 59 S.E.2d 168 (1950); Gilliland & Gaffney v. Southern Ry., 85 S.C. 26, 67 S.E. 20 (1910) (business).

Section (b)(7) is consistent with South Carolina law. State v. Pearson, 223 S.C. 377, 76 S.E.2d 151 (1953); Ex parte Steen, 59 S.C. 220, 37 S.E. 829 (1901). As to the authentication of police fingerprint records, see State v. Rich, 293 S.C. 172, 359 S.E.2d 281 (1987).

Subsection (b)(8) is in accord with prior case law with the exception that the prior cases required 30 years before a document was classified as ancient rather than 20 years as required by this subsection. See Atlantic Coast Line Ry. v. Searson, 137 S.C. 468, 135 S.E. 567 (1926); Polson v. Ingram, 22 S.C. 541 (1885); Thompson v. Brannon, 14 S.C. 542 (1881); Johnson v. Pritchard, 302 S.C. 437, 395 S.E.2d 191 (Ct. App. 1990). See also, Rule 803(16), which also reduces the minimum period for receipt of "ancient" records under the hearsay rule.

Subsection (b)(9) appears to be in accord with South Carolina law. See State v. Hester, 137 S.C. 145, 134 S.E.2d 885 (1926).

Subsection (b)(10) is the federal rule modified to make the language applicable to South Carolina statutes and rules. An example of such a rule is Rule 44, SCRCP, which deals with the authentication of official records.

RULE 902. SELF-AUTHENTICATION

Extrinsic evidence of authenticity as a condition precedent to admissibility is not required with respect to the following:

(1) Domestic Public Documents Under Seal. A document bearing a seal purporting to be that of the United States, or of any State, district, Commonwealth, territory, or insular possession thereof, or the Panama Canal Zone, or the Trust Territory of the Pacific Islands, or of a political subdivision, department, officer, or agency thereof, and a signature purporting to be an attestation or execution.

(2) Domestic Public Documents Not Under Seal. A document purporting to bear the signature in the official capacity of an officer or employee of any entity included in subsection (1) hereof, having no seal, if a public officer having a seal and having official duties in the district or political subdivision of the officer or employee certifies under seal that the signer has the official capacity and that the signature is genuine.

(3) Foreign Public Documents. A document purporting to be executed or attested in an official capacity by a person authorized by the laws of a foreign country to make the execution or attestation, and accompanied by a final certification as to the genuineness of the signature and official position (A) of the executing or attesting person, or (B) of any foreign official whose certificate of genuineness of signature and official position relates to the execution or attestation or is in a chain of certificates of genuineness of signature and official position relating to the execution or attestation. A final certification may be made by a secretary of embassy or legation, consul general, consul, vice consul, or consular agent of the United States, or a diplomatic or consular official of the foreign country assigned or accredited to the United States. If reasonable opportunity has been given to all parties to investigate the authenticity and accuracy of official documents, the court may, for good cause shown, order that they be treated as presumptively authentic without final certification or permit them to be evidenced by an attested summary with or without final certification.

(4) Certified Copies of Public Records. A copy of an official record or report or entry therein, or of a document authorized by law to be recorded or filed and actually recorded or filed in a public office, including data compilations in any form, certified as correct by the custodian or other person authorized to make the certification, by certificate complying with subsection (1), (2), or (3) of this rule or complying with any statute or rule promulgated by the Supreme Court.

(5) Official Publications. Books, pamphlets, or other publications purporting to be issued by public authority.

(6) Newspapers and Periodicals. Printed materials purporting to be newspapers or periodicals.

(7) Trade Inscriptions and the Like. Inscriptions, signs, tags, or labels purporting to have been affixed in the course of business and indicating ownership, control, or origin.

(8) Acknowledged Documents. Documents accompanied by a certificate of acknowledgment executed in the manner provided by law by a notary public or other officer authorized by law to take acknowledgments.

(9) Commercial Paper and Related Documents. Commercial paper, signatures thereon, and documents relating thereto to the extent provided by general commercial law.

(10) Presumptions Under Statutes. Any signature, document or other matter declared by statute to be presumptively or prima facie genuine or authentic.

Note:
With the exception of subsections (4) and (10) which are discussed below, this rule is identical to the federal rule.

Subsection (1): South Carolina law has previously permitted self-authentication of certain classes of domestic public documents under seal. See e.g., S.C. Code Ann. § 19-5-220 (1985) (proof of various documents under seal of any city or state).

Subsection (2): There does not appear to be any South Carolina law permitting self-authentication in these circumstances.

Subsection (3) is similar to Rule 44(a)(2), SCRCP.

Subsection (4) is identical to the federal rule except that it is amended so as to also allow compliance with "any statute or rule prescribed by the Supreme Court." Examples of such statutes and rules include: S.C. Code Ann. § 19-5-10 (1985) (admissibility of certified copies or certified photostatic copies of documents); S.C. Code Ann. § 19-5-30 (Supp. 1993) (admissibility of photostatic or certified copies of certain motor vehicle records); Rule 44(a)(1), SCRCP (authentication of domestic records); Rule 6, SCRCrimP (self-authentication of chemist's or analyst's report of nature of "controlled dangerous substances").

Subsection (5): There does not appear to be any South Carolina authority for this proposition.

Subsection (6) appears to be consistent with South Carolina law. See Kirkpatrick v. Hardeman, 123 S.C. 21, 115 S.E. 905 (1923) (although unclear if Court treated as hearsay or authentication problem, newspaper reports of stock quotations were admitted for purpose of proving market value of stock).

Subsection (7): There does not appear to be any South Carolina authority for this proposition.

Subsection (8): This is similar to South Carolina Code Ann. §§ 19-5-220 and 19-5-230 (1985) which allow the self-authentication of certain documents of city, state or foreign governments under seal of a notary public.

Subsection (9): Under the Uniform Commercial Code, certain items are self-authenticating. See S.C. Code Ann. § 36-1-202 (1976) (includes bills of lading, insurance policies or any document authorized by the contract to be issued by third party); § 36-3-307 (1976) (signatures, unless specifically denied in the pleadings); § 36-3-510 (1976) (formal certificate of protest, a stamp by drawee that payment was refused, or bank records showing dishonor are all admissible in evidence and create a presumption of dishonor); § 36-8-105(3) (Supp. 1993) (signatures on a certificated security, in a necessary indorsement, on an initial transaction statement or on an instruction is admitted unless put into issue).

Subsection (10): This subsection differs from the federal rule only in that "declared by statute" is substituted for "declared by Act of Congress." An example of a statute under this subsection is S.C. Code Ann. § 39-15-140 (1985) (certificate of trademark registration issued by the Secretary of State).

RULE 903. SUBSCRIBING WITNESS' TESTIMONY UNNECESSARY

The testimony of a subscribing witness is not necessary to authenticate a writing unless required by statute or by the laws of the jurisdiction whose laws govern the validity of the writing.

Note:

This rule adds "by statute" to the federal rule. The law in South Carolina is that the testimony of a subscribing witness is generally not necessary for authentication. Edgar v. Brown, 15 S.C.L. (4 McCord) 91 (1827); S.C. Code Ann. § 19-1-120 (1985) (the absence of a witness to any bond or note shall not be deemed a good cause by any court for postponing a trial, but the signature may be proved by other testimony); S.C. Code Ann. § 62-2-503 (Supp. 1993) (Uniform Probate Code's provision for self-proved wills); §§ 62-3-405 and -406 (Supp. 1993) (requirements of proof of execution when will not self-proved and submitted for formal probate).

Article X. Contents of Writings, Recordings, and Photographs

RULE 1001. DEFINITIONS

For purposes of this article the following definitions are applicable:

(1) Writings and Recordings. "Writings" and "recordings" consist of letters, words, sounds, or numbers, or their equivalent, set down by handwriting, typewriting, printing, Photostatting, photographing, magnetic impulse, mechanical or electronic recording, or other form of data compilation.

(2) Photographs. "Photographs" include still photographs, X-ray films, video tapes, motion pictures or other similar methods of recording information.

(3) Original. An "original" of a writing or recording is the writing or recording itself or any counterpart intended to have the same effect by a person executing or issuing it. An "original" of a photograph includes the negative or any print therefrom. If data are stored in a computer or similar device, any printout or other output readable by sight, shown to reflect the data accurately, is an "original".

(4) Duplicate. A "duplicate" is a counterpart produced by the same impression as the original, or from the same matrix, or by means of photography, including enlargements and miniatures, or by mechanical or electronic re-recording, or by chemical reproduction, or by other equivalent techniques which accurately reproduces the original.

Note:
This rule is identical to the federal rule except that the word "sounds" is added to subdivision (1) and "other similar methods of recording information" was added to subdivision (2). This additional language does not significantly alter the rule, and provides for advances in technology.

RULE 1002. REQUIREMENT OF ORIGINAL

To prove the content of a writing, recording, or photograph, the original writing, recording, or photograph is required, except as otherwise provided in these rules or by statute.

Note:

This rule is better known as the best evidence rule. This rule is identical to the federal rule except the words "by statute" were substituted at the end of the rule in place of the words "by Act of Congress."

The proposed rule is consistent with current case law as it applies to writings. See, e.g., Riddle v. City of Greenville, 251 S.C. 473, 163 S.E.2d 462 (1968); Sample v. Gulf Refining Co., 183 S.C. 399, 191 S.E. 209 (1937); Cain v. Whitlock, 178 S.C. 289, 182 S.E. 752 (1935); Mull v. Easley Lumber Co., 121 S.C. 155, 113 S.E. 356 (1922); Guinarin v. So. Life & Trust Co., 106 S.C. 37, 90 S.E. 319 (1916); Mayfield v. So. Ry., 85 S.C. 165, 67 S.E. 132 (1910); McCoy v. Atl. Coast Line Ry., 84 S.C. 62, 65 S.E. 939 (1909).

There are no cases which deal with the applicability of the best evidence rule to photographs and only one case in which the best evidence rule has been applied to recordings. State v. Worthy, 239 S.C. 449, 123 S.E.2d 835 (1962), overruled on other grounds, State v. Torrence, 305 S.C. 45, 406 S.E.2d 315 (1991).

Examples of statutes that have an effect on the requirement to produce the original are: S.C. Code Ann. § 19-1-110 (1985) (instruments of common carriers); S.C. Code Ann. § 19-5-10 (1985) (public documents); S.C. Code Ann. § 19-5-210 (1985) (grants issued by North Carolina); S.C. Code Ann. §§ 19-5-310 and -320 (1985) (missing person reports); S.C. Code Ann. § 19-5-510 (1985) (business records).

RULE 1003. ADMISSIBILITY OF DUPLICATES

A duplicate is admissible to the same extent as an original unless (1) a genuine question is raised as to the authenticity of the original or (2) in the circumstances it would be unfair to admit the duplicate in lieu of the original.

Note:

This rule is identical to the federal rule. There is no case law in this State on the admissibility of a duplicate in this context, only on the admissibility of a duplicate as secondary evidence. See Note following Rule 1004.

RULE 1004. ADMISSIBILITY OF OTHER EVIDENCE OF CONTENTS

The original is not required, and other evidence of the contents of a writing, recording, or photograph is admissible if -

(1) Originals Lost or Destroyed. All originals are lost or have been destroyed, unless the proponent lost or destroyed them in bad faith; or

(2) Original Not Obtainable. No original can be obtained by any available judicial process or procedure; or

(3) Original in Possession of Opponent. At a time when an original was under the control of the party against whom offered, that party was put on notice, by the pleadings or otherwise, that the contents would be a subject of proof at the hearing, and that party does not produce the original at the hearing; or

(4) Collateral Matters. The writing, recording, or photograph is not closely related to a controlling issue.

Note:

This rule is identical to the federal rule and is consistent with our case law. It has long been the law in South Carolina that secondary evidence is admissible under the circumstances outlined in this rule. See, e.g., Pee

Dee Prod. Credit Ass'n v. Love, 284 S.C. 371, 326 S.E.2d 650 (1984) (original lost); Windham v. Lloyd, 253 S.C. 568, 172 S.E.2d 117 (1970) (original lost); Wynn v. Coney, 232 S.C. 346, 102 S.E.2d 209 (1958) (original in possession of opponent); Greer v. Equitable Life Assur. Soc'y, 180 S.C. 162, 185 S.E. 68 (1936) (collateral matter); Rose v. Winnsboro Nat'l Bank, 41 S.C. 191, 19 S.E. 487 (1894) (original in possession of opponent).

RULE 1005. PUBLIC RECORDS

The contents of an official record, or of a document authorized to be recorded or filed and actually recorded or filed, including data compilations in any form, if otherwise admissible, may be proved by copy, certified as correct in accordance with Rule 902 or testified to be correct by a witness who has compared it with the original. If a copy which complies with the foregoing cannot be obtained by the exercise of reasonable diligence, then other evidence of the contents may be given.

Note:
This rule is identical to the federal rule and is substantially similar to S.C. Code Ann. § 19-5-10 (1985) and Rule 44, SCRCP.

RULE 1006. SUMMARIES

The contents of voluminous writings, recordings, or photographs which cannot conveniently be examined in court may be presented in the form of a chart, summary, or calculation, provided the underlying data are admissible into evidence. The originals, or duplicates, shall be made available for examination or copying, or both, by other parties at reasonable time and place. The court may order that they be produced in court.

Note:
This rule is identical to the federal rule except for the language "provided the underlying data are admissible into evidence" and is consistent with South Carolina case law. Adamson v. Marianne Fabrics, Inc., 301 S.C. 204, 391 S.E.2d 249 (1990); Zemp Constr. Co. v. Harmon Bros. Constr.

Co., 225 S.C. 361, 82 S.E.2d 531 (1954); Crowley v. Spivey, 285 S.C. 397, 329 S.E.2d 774 (Ct. App.1985); Butler v. Sea Pines Plantation Co., 282 S.C. 113, 317 S.E.2d 464 (Ct. App.1984). It should be noted that the case of Pegler v. Atlantic Coast Line R.R., 234 S.C. 140, 107 S.E.2d 15 (1959), is inconsistent with these prior cases and has been effectively overruled.

RULE 1007. TESTIMONY OR WRITTEN ADMISSION OF PARTY

Contents of writings, recordings, or photographs may be proved by the testimony or deposition of the party against whom offered or by that party's written admission, without accounting for the nonproduction of the original.

Note:

This rule is identical to the federal rule. The case law has not previously recognized any limitation on the form of the statement or admission which can be used. Gardner v. City of Columbia Police Dep't, 216 S.C. 219, 57 S.E.2d 308 (1950). Therefore, this rule may be somewhat narrower since it limits the statements or admissions which can be used to those contained in testimony, deposition or written admission.

RULE 1008. FUNCTIONS OF COURT AND JURY

When the admissibility of other evidence of contents of writings, recordings, or photographs under these rules depends upon the fulfillment of a condition of fact, the question whether the condition has been fulfilled is ordinarily for the court to determine in accordance with the provisions of Rule 104. However, when an issue is raised (a) whether the asserted writing even existed, or (b) whether another writing, recording, or photograph produced at the trial is the original, or (c) whether other evidence of contents correctly reflects the contents, the issue is for the trier of fact to determine as in the case of other issues of fact.

Note:

This rule is identical to the federal rule. It has long been held in this State that a question as to whether to admit a document under the best evidence rule is addressed to the discretion of the trial judge. Shirer v. O.W.S. & Associates, 253 S.C. 232, 169 S.E.2d 621 (1969); Vaught v. Nationwide Mut. Ins. Co., 250 S.C. 65, 156 S.E.2d 627 (1967); Drayton v. Industrial Life & Health Ins. Co., 205 S.C. 98, 31 S.E.2d 148 (1944); Sample v. Gulf Refining Co., 183 S.C. 399, 191 S.E. 209 (1937); Atlantic Coast Line R.R. v. Dawes, 103 S.C. 507, 88 S.E. 286 (1916); Leesville Mfg. Co. v. Morgan Wood & Iron Works, 75 S.C. 342, 55 S.E. 768 (1906); Wayne Smith Constr. Co., Inc. v. Wolman, Duberstein, and Thompson, 294 S.C. 140, 363 S.E.2d 115 (Ct. App. 1987). There are no cases discussing the role of the trier of fact in this area.

Article XI. Miscellaneous Rules

RULE 1101. APPLICABILITY OF RULES

(a) Courts and Judges. Except as otherwise provided by rule or statute, these rules apply to the courts of South Carolina. The term "judge" in these rules includes justices of the Supreme Court; judges of the Court of Appeals; judges of the circuit, family, probate and municipal courts; magistrates; masters-in-equity; and special referees.

(b) Proceedings Generally. These rules apply generally to civil actions and proceedings, to criminal cases and proceedings, and to contempt proceedings except those in which the court may act summarily.

(c) Rule of Privilege. The rule with respect to privileges applies at all stages of all actions, cases, and proceedings.

(d) Rules Inapplicable. The rules (other than with respect to privileges) do not apply in the following situations:

(1) Preliminary Questions of Fact. The determination of questions of fact preliminary to admissibility of evidence when the issue is to be determined by the court under Rule 104.

(2) Grand Jury. Proceedings before grand juries.

(3) Miscellaneous Proceedings. Proceedings for extradition; preliminary hearings in criminal cases; sentencing (except in the penalty phase of capital trials as required by statute), dispositional hearings in juvenile delinquency matters, or granting or revoking probation; issuance of warrants for arrest, criminal summonses, and search warrants; and proceedings with respect to release on bail or otherwise.

Note:
Except for subsections (a), (b), and (d)(3), this rule is identical to the federal rule.

In subsection (a), the federal rule has been amended by adding the phrase "except as otherwise provided by rule or statute." See Note to

Rule 101. Further, the phrase "courts of South Carolina" replaces the list of courts in the federal rule, and the term "judge" is modified to include all levels of the unified judiciary. These changes emphasize the fact that these rules are applicable to all levels of the unified judiciary.

Subsection (b) indicates that these rules apply generally to all civil and criminal proceedings except for summary criminal contempt. This exception is consistent with the relaxed procedural requirements for the imposition of summary contempt. Cf. State v. Weinberg, 229 S.C. 286, 92 S.E.2d 842 (1956).

Regarding subsection (c), no South Carolina authority has been found to support the proposition that the rules of privilege remain applicable even if the other rules of evidence are inapplicable.

Regarding subsection (d)(1), no South Carolina authority has been found regarding this proposition.

Subsection (d)(2) is consistent with the case law in South Carolina. See State v. Williams, 301 S.C. 369, 392 S.E.2d 181 (1990) (the validity of an indictment is not affected by the character of the evidence considered by the grand jury and, if valid on its face, the indictment may not be challenged on the ground that the grand jury acted on the basis of incompetent evidence); State v. Williams, 263 S.C. 290, 210 S.E.2d 298 (1974) (a grand jury indictment is not subject to dismissal on the basis that it was founded upon hearsay evidence).

To be consistent with the terminology used in this State, the phrase "preliminary hearings" in subsection (d)(3) replaces the phrase "preliminary examinations" in the federal rule. In addition, the phrase "dispositional hearings in juvenile delinquency matters" has been added to subsection (d)(3). Although no cases have been found regarding the application of the rules of evidence to extradition proceedings, subsection (d)(3) is generally consistent with prior law in this State. See State v. Dingle, 279 S.C. 278, 306 S.E.2d 223 (1983) (rules concerning hearsay inapplicable in preliminary hearings); State v. Franklin, 267 S.C. 240, 226 S.E.2d 896 (1976) (before imposing a sentence, judge may appropriately conduct an inquiry largely unlimited either as to the kind of information he may consider or the source from which it may come); State v. Sullivan, 267 S.C. 610, 230 S.E.2d 621 (1967) (a search warrant may be issued on an affidavit even when the affidavit is based on hearsay statements); State v. Hill, 5 S.C.L. (3 Brev.) 89, 6 S.C.L. (1 Tread.) 242 (1812) (the court may hear and consider affidavits when determining whether to admit a defendant to bail). However, as to probation revocation, the rule may constitute a change in the law. See State v. White, 218 S.C. 130, 61 S.E.2d 754 (1950) (hearsay rules applied in review of probation revocation).

RULE 1102. AMENDMENTS

Amendments to the South Carolina Rules of Evidence may be made by the South Carolina Supreme Court.

Note:
This is the federal rule modified to apply to South Carolina.

RULE 1103. TITLE AND EFFECTIVE DATE

(a) Title. These rules shall be entitled South Carolina Rules of Evidence, and may be cited by rule number and the letters SCRE, i.e., Rule ____, SCRE.

(b) Effective Date. These rules shall become effective September 3, 1995.

Note:
The language of subsection (a) is based on Rule 85(a), SCRCP. The federal rules do not contain a counterpart to subsection (b).

www.ingramcontent.com/pod-product-compliance
Lightning Source LLC
Chambersburg PA
CBHW081454220526
45466CB00008B/2641